· AESCHYLUS ·

AGAMEMNON

TRANSLATED INTO

ENGLISH RHYMING VERSE

WITH

EXPLANATORY NOTES

By GILBERT MURRAY

Regius Professor of Greek
the University of Oxford

OXFORD UNIVERSITY PRESS

NEW YORK LONDON TORONTO

1939

PREFACE

THE sense of difficulty, and indeed of awe, with which a scholar approaches the task of translating the *Agamemnon* depends directly on its greatness as poetry. It is in part a matter of diction. The language of Aeschylus is an extraordinary thing, the syntax stiff and simple, the vocabulary obscure, unexpected, and steeped in splendour. Its peculiarities cannot be disregarded, or the translation will be false in character. Yet not Milton himself could produce in English the same great music, and a translator who should strive ambitiously to represent the complex effect of the original would clog his own powers of expression and strain his instrument to breaking. But, apart from the diction in this narrower sense, there is a quality of atmosphere surrounding the *Agamemnon* which seems almost to defy reproduction in another setting, because it depends in large measure on the position of the play in the historical development of Greek literature.

If we accept the view that all Art to some extent, and Greek tragedy in a very special degree, moves in its course of development from Religion to Entertainment, from a Service to a Performance, the *Agamemnon* seems to stand at a critical point where the balance of the two elements is near perfection. The drama has come fully to life, but the religion has not yet faded to a formality. The *Agamemnon* is not, like Aeschylus' *Suppliant Women,* a statue half-hewn out of the rock. It is a real play, showing clash of character and situation, suspense and movement, psychological depth and subtlety. Yet it still remains something more than a play. Its atmosphere is not quite of this world. In the long lyrics especially one feels that the guiding emotion is not the entertainer's wish to thrill an audience, not even perhaps the pure artist's wish to create beauty, but something deeper and more prophetic, a passionate contemplation and expression of truth; though of course the truth in question is something felt rather than stated, something that pervades life, an eternal and majestic rhythm like the movement of the stars.

Thus, if Longinus is right in defining Sublimity as " the ring, or resonance, of greatness of soul," one sees in part where the sublimity of the *Agamemnon* comes from. And it is worth noting that the faults which some critics have found in the play are in harmony with this conclusion. For the sublimity that is rooted in religion tolerates some faults and utterly refuses to tolerate others. The *Agamemnon* may be slow in getting to work; it may be stiff with antique conventions. It never approaches to being cheap or insincere or shallow or sentimental or showy. It never ceases to be genuinely a " criticism of life." The theme which it treats, for instance, is a great theme in its own right; it is not a made-up story ingeniously handled.

The trilogy of the *Oresteia,* of which this play is the first part, centres on the old and everlastingly unsolved problem of

The ancient blinded vengeance and the wrong that amendeth wrong.

Every wrong is justly punished; yet, as the world goes, every punishment becomes a new wrong, calling for fresh vengeance. And more; every wrong turns out to be itself rooted in some wrong of old. It is never gratuitous, never untempted by the working of Peitho (Persuasion), never merely wicked. The *Oresteia* first shows the cycle of crime punished by crime which must be repunished, and then seeks for some gleam of escape, some breaking of the endless chain of "evil duty." In the old order of earth and heaven there was no such escape. Each blow called for the return blow and must do so *ad infinitum*. But, according to Aeschylus, there is a new Ruler now in heaven, one who has both sinned and suffered and thereby grown wise. He is Zeus the Third Power, Zeus the Saviour, and his gift to mankind is the ability through suffering to Learn (pp. 7 f.)

At the opening of the *Agamemnon* we find Clytemnestra alienated from her husband and secretly befriended with his ancestral enemy, Aigisthos. The air is heavy and throbbing with hate; hate which is evil but has its due cause. Agamemnon, obeying the prophet Calchas, when the fleet lay storm-bound at Aulis, had given his own daughter, Iphigenîa, as a human sacrifice. And if we ask how a sane man had consented to such an act, we are told of his gradual temptation; the deadly excuse offered by ancient superstition; and above all, the fact that he had already inwardly accepted the great whole of which this horror was a part. At the first outset of his expedition against Troy there had appeared an omen, the bloody sign of two eagles devouring a mother-hare with her unborn young. . . . The question was thus put to the Kings and their prophet: Did they or did they not accept the sign, and wish to be those Eagles? And they had answered Yes. They would have their vengeance, their full and extreme victory, and were ready to pay the price. The sign once accepted, the prophet recoils from the consequences which, in prophetic vision, he sees following therefrom: but the decision has been taken, and the long tale of cruelty rolls on, culminating in the triumphant sack of Troy, which itself becomes not an assertion of Justice but a whirlwind of godless destruction. And through all these doings of fierce beasts and angry men the unseen Pity has been alive and watching, the Artemis who " abhors the Eagles' feast," the " Apollo or Pan or Zeus " who hears the crying of the robbed vulture; nay, if even the Gods were deaf, the mere " wrong of the dead " at Troy might waken, groping for some retribution upon the " Slayer of Many Men " (pp. 15, 20).

If we ask why men are so blind, seeking their welfare thus through incessant evil, Aeschylus will tell us that the cause lies in the infection of old sin, old cruelty. There is no doubt somewhere a $\pi\rho\acute{\omega}\tau\alpha\rho\chi os\,{}^{"}A\tau\eta$, a " first blind deed of wrong," but in practice every wrong is the result of another. And the Children of Atreus are steeped to the lips in them. When the prophetess Cassandra, out of her first vague horror at the evil House, begins to grope towards some definite image, first and most haunting comes the sound of the weeping of two little children, murdered long ago, in a feud that was not theirs. From that point, more than any other, the Daemon or Genius of the House—more than its " Luck," a little less than its Guardian Angel—becomes an Alastor or embodied Curse, a " Red Slayer " which cries ever for peace and cleansing, but can seek them only in the same blind way, through vengeance, and, when that fails, then through more vengeance (p. 69).

This awful conception of a race intent upon its own wrongs, and blindly groping towards the very terror it is trying to avoid, is typified, as it were, in the Cassandra story. That daughter of Priam was beloved by Apollo, who gave her the power of true prophecy. In some way that we know not, she broke her promise to the God; and, since his gift could not be recalled, he added to it the curse that, while she should always foresee and foretell the truth, none should believe her. The Cassandra scene is a creation beyond praise or criticism. The old scholiast speaks of the " pity and amazement " which it causes. The Elders who talk with her wish to believe, they try to understand, they are really convinced of Cassandra's powers. But the curse is too strong. The special thing which Cassandra tries again and again to say always eludes them, and they can raise no finger to prevent the disaster happening. And when it does happen they are, as they have described themselves, weak and very old, " dreams wandering in the daylight."

The characters of this play seem, in a sense, to arise out of the theme and consequently to have, amid all their dramatic solidity, a further significance which is almost symbolic. Cassandra is, as it were, the incarnation of that knowledge which Herodotus describes as the crown of sorrow, the knowledge which sees and warns and cannot help (Hdt. ix. 16). Agamemnon himself, the King of Kings, triumphant and doomed, is a symbol of pride and the fall of pride. We must not think of him as bad or specially cruel. The watchman loved him (ll. 34 f.), and the lamentations of the Elders over his death have a note of personal affection (pp. 66 ff.). But I suspect that Aeschylus, a believer in the mystic meaning of names, took the name Agamemnon to be a warning that Ἄγα μίμνει, "the unseen Wrath abides." *Agâ*, of course, is not exactly wrath; it is more like Nemesis, the feeling that something is ἄγαν, "too much," the condemnation of *Hubris* (pride or overgrowth) and of all things that are in excess. *Agâ* is sometimes called "the jealousy of God," but such a translation is not happy. It is not the jealousy, nor even the indignation, of a personal God, but the profound repudiation and reversal of Hubris which is the very law of the Cosmos. Through all the triumph of the conqueror, this *Agâ* abides.

The greatest and most human character of the whole play is Clytemnestra. She is conceived on the grand Aeschylean scale, a scale which makes even Lady Macbeth and Beatrice Cenci seem small; she is more the kinswoman of Brynhild. Yet she is full not only of character, but of subtle psychology. She is the first and leading example of that time-honoured ornament of the tragic stage, the sympathetic, or semi-sympathetic, heroine-criminal. Aeschylus employs none of the devices of later playwrights to make her interesting. He admits, of course, no approach to a love-scene; he uses no sophisms; but he does make us see through Clytemnestra's eyes and feel through her passions. The agony of silent prayer in which, if my conception is right, we first see her, helps to interpret her speeches when they come; but every speech needs close study. She dare not speak sincerely or show her real feelings until Agamemnon is dead; and then she is practically a mad woman.

For I think here that there is a point which has not been observed. It is that Clytemnestra is conceived as being really " possessed " by the Daemon of the House when she commits her crime. Her statements on p. 69 are not empty metaphor. A careful study of the scene after the murder will show that she appears first " possessed " and almost insane with triumph, utterly dominating the Elders and leaving them no power to answer. Then gradually the unnatural force dies out from her. The deed that was first an ecstasy of delight becomes an " affliction " (pp. 72, 76). The strength that defied the world flags and changes into a longing for peace. She has done her work. She has purified the House of its madness; now let her go away and live out her life in quiet. When Aigisthos appears, and the scene suddenly becomes filled with the wrangling of common men, Clytemnestra fades into a long silence, from which she only emerges at the very end of the drama to pray again for Peace, and, strangest of all, to utter the entreaty: " Let us not stain ourselves with blood! " The splash of her husband's blood was visible on her face at the time. Had she in her trance-like state actually forgotten, or did she, even then, not feel that particular blood to be a stain?

To some readers it will seem a sort of irrelevance, or at least a blurring of the dramatic edge of this tragedy, to observe that the theme on which it is founded was itself the central theme both of Greek

Tragedy and of Greek Religion. The fall of Pride, the avenging of wrong by wrong, is no new subject selected by Aeschylus. It forms both the commonest burden of the moralising lyrics in Greek tragedy and even of the tragic myths themselves; and recent writers have shown how the same idea touches the very heart of the traditional Greek religion. "The life of the Year-Daemon, who lies at the root of so many Greek gods and heroes, is normally a story of Pride and Punishment. Each year arrives, waxes great, commits the sin of Hubris and must therefore die. It is the way of all Life. As an early philosopher expresses it, "All things pay retribution for their injustice one to another according to the ordinance of Time." [1]

To me this consideration actually increases the interest and beauty of the *Oresteia,* because it increases its greatness. The majestic art, the creative genius, the instinctive eloquence of these plays—that eloquence which is the mere despair of a translator—are all devoted to the expression of something which Aeschylus felt to be of tremendous import. It was not his discovery; but it was a truth of which he had an intense realization. It had become something which he must with all his strength bring to expression before he died, not in a spirit of self-assertion or of argument, like a discoverer, but as one devoted to something higher and greater than himself, in the spirit of an interpreter or prophet.

[1] See my *Four Stages of Greek Religion,* p. 47. Cornford, *From Religion to Philosophy,* Chapter I. See also the fine pages on the Agamemnon in the same writer's *Thucydides Mythistoricus,* pp. 144, ff. (E. Arnold 1907).

G. M.

AGAMEMNON

CHARACTERS IN THE PLAY

AGAMEMNON, *son of Atreus and King of Argos and Mycenae;
Commander-in-Chief of the Greek armies in the War
against Troy.*
CLYTEMNESTRA, daughter *of Tyndareus, sister of Helen; wife
to Agamemnon.*
AIGISTHOS, *son of Thyestes, cousin and blood-enemy to
Agamemnon, lover to Clytemnestra.*
CASSANDRA, *daughter of Priam, King of Troy, a prophetess;
now slave to Agamemnon.*
A WATCHMAN.
A HERALD.
CHORUS of Argive Elders, faithful to AGAMEMNON.

CHARACTERS MENTIONED IN THE PLAY

MENELÂÜS, *brother to Agamemnon, husband of Helen, and
King of Sparta. The two sons of Atreus are called
the Atreidae.*
HELEN, *most beautiful of women; daughter of Tyndareus,
wife to* MENELÂÜS; *beloved and carried off by Paris.*
PARIS, *son of Priam, King of Troy, lover of Helen. Also
called* ALEXANDER.
PRIAM, *the aged King of Troy.*

*The Greeks are also referred to as Achaians, Argives,
Danaans; Troy is also called Ilion.*

*The play was produced in the archonship of Philocles
(458* B.C.*).*
*The first prize was won by Aeschylus with the " Agamem-
non," " Choëphoroe," " Eumenides," and the Satyr Play
" Proteus."*

THE AGAMEMNON

The Scene represents a space in front of the Palace of Agamemnon in Argos, with an Altar of Zeus in the centre and many other altars at the sides. On a high terrace of the roof stands a WATCHMAN. *It is night.*

WATCHMAN.

THIS waste of year-long vigil I have prayed
God for some respite, watching elbow-stayed,
As sleuthhounds watch, above the Atreidae's hall,
Till well I know yon midnight festival
Of swarming stars, and them that lonely go,
Bearers to man of summer and of snow,
Great lords and shining, throned in heavenly fire.
  And still I await the sign, the beacon pyre
That bears Troy's capture on a voice of flame
Shouting o'erseas. So surely to her aim
Cleaveth a woman's heart, man-passionèd!
And when I turn me to my bed—my bed
Dew-drenched and dark and stumbling, to which near
Cometh no dream nor sleep, but alway Fear
Breathes round it, warning, lest an eye once fain
To close may close too well to wake again;
Think I perchance to sing or troll a tune
For medicine against sleep, the music soon

Changes to sighing for the tale untold
Of this house, not well mastered as of old.

   Howbeit, may God yet send us rest, and light
The flame of good news flashed across the night.

> [*He is silent, watching. Suddenly at a distance in*
> *the night there is a glimmer of fire, increasing*
> *presently to a blaze.*

Ha!
O kindler of the dark, O daylight birth
Of dawn and dancing upon Argive earth
For this great end! All hail!—What ho, within!
What ho! Bear word to Agamemnon's queen
To rise, like dawn, and lift in answer strong
To this glad lamp her women's triumph-song,
If verily, verily, Ilion's citadel
Is fallen, as yon beacons flaming tell.

   And I myself will tread the dance before
All others; for my master's dice I score
Good, and mine own to-night three sixes plain.

> [*Lights begin to show in the Palace.*

Oh, good or ill, my hand shall clasp again
My dear lord's hand, returning! Beyond that
I speak not. A great ox hath laid his weight
Across my tongue. But these stone walls know well,
If stones had speech, what tale were theirs to tell.
For me, to him that knoweth I can yet
Speak; if another questions I forget.

> [*Exit into the Palace. The women's " Ololûgê,"*
> *or triumph-cry, is heard within and then*
> *repeated again and again further off in*
> *the City. Handmaids and Attendants come*

from the Palace, bearing torches, with which
they kindle incense on the altars. Among
them comes CLYTEMNESTRA, *who throws*
herself on her knees at the central Altar in
an agony of prayer.

Presently from the further side of the open
space appear the CHORUS *of* ELDERS *and*
move gradually into position in front of the
Palace. The day begins to dawn.

CHORUS.

Ten years since Ilion's righteous foes,
  The Atreidae strong,
Menelaüs and eke Agamemnon arose,
Two thrones, two sceptres, yokèd of God;
And a thousand galleys of Argos trod
  The seas for the righting of wrong;
And wrath of battle about them cried,
    As vultures cry,
Whose nest is plundered, and up they fly
In anguish lonely, eddying wide,
Great wings like oars in the waste of sky,
Their task gone from them, no more to keep
Watch o'er the vulture babes asleep.
But One there is who heareth on high
Some Pan or Zeus, some lost Apollo—
That keen bird-throated suffering cry
Of the stranger wronged in God's own sky;
And sendeth down, for the law transgressed,
  The Wrath of the Feet that follow.

So Zeus the Watcher of Friend and Friend,
Zeus who Prevaileth, in after quest

For One Belovèd by Many Men
On Paris sent the Atreidae twain;
Yea, sent him dances before the end
          For his bridal cheer,
Wrestlings heavy and limbs forespent
For Greek and Trojan, the knee earth-bent,
The bloody dust and the broken spear.
He knoweth, that which is here is here,
And that which Shall Be followeth near;
He seeketh God with a great desire,
He heaps his gifts, he essays his pyre
With torch below and with oil above,
With tears, but never the wrath shall move
Of the Altar cold that rejects his fire.

We saw the Avengers go that day,
And they left us here; for our flesh is old
And serveth not; and these staves uphold
A strength like the strength of a child at play.
For the sap that springs in the young man's hand
And the valour of age, they have left the land.
And the passing old, while the dead leaf blows
And the old staff gropeth his three-foot way,
Weak as a babe and alone he goes,
A dream left wandering in the day.

[*Coming near the Central Altar they see* CLY-
TEMNESTRA, *who is still rapt in prayer.*

But thou, O daughter of Tyndareus,
Queen Clytemnestra, what need? What news?
What tale or tiding hath stirred thy mood
To send forth word upon all our ways
For incensed worship? Of every god

That guards the city, the deep, the high,
Gods of the mart, gods of the sky,
    The altars blaze.
    One here, one there,
To the skyey night the firebrands flare,
Drunk with the soft and guileless spell
Of balm of kings from the inmost cell.
Tell, O Queen, and reject us not,
All that can or that may be told,
And healer be to this aching thought,
Which one time hovereth, evil-cold,
And then from the fires thou kindlest
Will Hope be kindled, and hungry Care
Fall back for a little while, nor tear
The heart that beateth below my breast.

[CLYTEMNESTRA *rises silently, as though uncon-
    scious of their presence, and goes into the
    House. The* CHORUS *take position and be-
    gin their first Stasimon, or Standing-song.*

CHORUS.

(*The sign seen on the way; Eagles tearing a hare
    with young.*)

It is ours to tell of the Sign of the War-way given,
    To men more strong,
(For a life that is kin unto ours yet breathes from
    heaven
    A spell, a Strength of Song:)
How the twin-throned Might of Achaia, one Crown
    divided
    Above all Greeks that are,

With avenging hand and spear upon Troy was guided
    By the Bird of War.
'Twas a King among birds to each of the Kings of
    the Sea,
  One Eagle black, one black but of fire-white tail,
By the House, on the Spear-hand, in station that all
    might see;
And they tore a hare, and the life in her womb that
    grew,
Yea, the life unlived and the races unrun they
    slew.
    Sorrow, sing sorrow: but good prevail, prevail!

(How Calchas read the sign; his Vision of the Future.)

And the War-seer wise, as he looked on the Atreïd
    Yoke
    Twain-tempered, knew
Those fierce hare-renders the lords of his host; and
    spoke,
    Reading the omen true.
" At the last, the last, this Hunt hunteth Ilion down,
    Yea, and before the wall
Violent division the fulness of land and town
    Shall waste withal;
If only God's eye gloom not against our gates,
  And the great War-curb of Troy, fore-smitten,
    fail.
For Pity lives, and those wingèd Hounds she hates,
  Which tore in the Trembler's body the unborn
    beast.
And Artemis abhorreth the eagles' feast."
    Sorrow, sing sorrow: but good prevail, prevail!

(He prays to Artemis to grant the fulfilment of the Sign, but, as his vision increases, he is afraid and calls on Paian, the Healer, to hold her back.)

" Thou beautiful One, thou tender lover
　　Of the dewy breath of the Lion's child ;
Thou the delight, through den and cover,
　　Of the young life at the breast of the wild,
Yet, oh, fulfill, fulfill　The sign of the Eagles' Kill !
Be the vision accepted, albeit horrible. . . .
But I-ê, I-ê!　Stay her, O Paian, stay !
For lo, upon other evil her heart she setteth,
　　Long wastes of wind, held ship and unventured sea,
On, on, till another Shedding of Blood be wrought :
They kill but feast not ; they pray not ; the law is
　　broken ;
Strife in the flesh, and the bride she obeyeth not,
And beyond, beyond, there abideth in wrath re-
　　awoken—
It plotteth, it haunteth the house, yea, it never for-
　　getteth—
　　Wrath for a child to be."
So Calchas, reading the wayside eagles' sign,
　　Spake to the Kings, blessings and words of bale ;
　　　And like his song be thine,
Sorrow, sing sorrow: but good prevail, prevail!

(Such religion belongs to old and barbarous gods, and brings no peace. I turn to Zeus, who has shown man how to Learn by Suffering.)
　　　Zeus ! Zeus, whate'er He be,
　　　If this name He love to hear
　　　This He shall be called of me.
　　　Searching earth and sea and air

Refuge nowhere can I find
Save Him only, if my mind
Will cast off before it die
The burden of this vanity.

One there was who reigned of old,
Big with wrath to brave and blast,
Lo, his name is no more told!
And who followed met at last
His Third-thrower, and is gone.
Only they whose hearts have known
Zeus, the Conqueror and the Friend,
They shall win their vision's end;

Zeus the Guide, who made man turn
Thought-ward, Zeus, who did ordain
Man by Suffering shall Learn.
So the heart of him, again
Aching with remembered pain,
Bleeds and sleepeth not, until
Wisdom comes against his will.
'Tis the gift of One by strife
Lifted to the throne of life.

(AGAMEMNON *accepted the sign. Then came long
delays and storm while the fleet lay at Aulis.*)

So that day the Elder Lord,
Marshal of the Achaian ships,
Strove not with the prophet's word,
Bowed him to his fate's eclipse,
When with empty jars and lips

Parched and seas impassable
Fate on that Greek army fell,
Fronting Chalcis as it lay,
By Aulis in the swirling bay.

(*Till at last Calchas answered that Artemis was wroth
and demanded the death of* AGAMEMNON'S *daughter. The King's doubt and grief.*)

And winds, winds   blew from Strymon River,
Unharboured, starving,   winds of waste endeavour,
Man-blinding, pitiless   to cord and bulwark,
   And the waste of days   was made long, more long,
Till the flower of Argos   was aghast and withered;
   Then through the storm   rose the War-seer's song,
And told of medicine   that should tame the tempest,
   But bow the Princes   to a direr wrong.
Then " Artemis " he whispered, he named the name;
And the brother Kings they shook in the hearts of
      them,
And smote on the earth their staves, and the tears
      came.

But the King, the elder,   hath found voice and
      spoken:
" A heavy doom, sure,   if God's will were broken;
But to slay mine own child,   who my house delighteth,
   Is that not heavy?   That her blood should flow
On her father's hand,   hard beside an altar?
   My path is sorrow   wheresoe'er I go.
Shall Agamemnon   fail his ships and people,
   And the hosts of Hellas   melt as melts the snow?
They cry, they thirst, for a death that shall break
      the spell,

For a Virgin's blood: 'tis a rite of old, men tell.
And they burn with longing.—O God may the end
   be well!"

(*But ambition drove him, till he consented to the sin of
   slaying his daughter, Iphigenia, as a sacrifice.*)

To the yoke of Must-Be   he bowed him slowly,
   And a strange wind   within his bosom tossed,
A wind of dark thought,   unclean, unholy;
   And he rose up, daring   to the uttermost.
For men are boldened   by a Blindness, straying
   Toward base desire,   which brings grief hereafter,
      Yea, and itself is grief;
So this man hardened   to his own child's slaying,
   As help to avenge him   for a woman's laughter
      And bring his ships relief!

Her "Father, Father,"   her sad cry that lingered,
   Her virgin heart's breath   they held all as naught,
Those bronze-clad witnesses   and battle-hungered;
   And there they prayed, and   when the prayer was
     wrought
He charged the young men   to uplift and bind her,
   As ye lift a wild kid,   high above the altar,
      Fierce-huddling forward,   fallen, clinging sore
To the robe that wrapt her; yea, he bids them hinder
   The sweet mouth's utterance,   the cries that falter,
     —His curse for evermore!—

With violence and a curb's voiceless wrath.
   Her stole of saffron then to the ground she threw,
And her eye with an arrow of pity found its path
     To each man's heart that slew:

A face in a picture, striving amazedly;
  The little maid who danced at her father's board,
The innocent voice man's love came never nigh,
Who joined to his her little paean-cry
    When the third cup was poured. . . .

What came thereafter I saw not neither tell.
  But the craft of Calchas failed not.—'Tis written, He
Who Suffereth Shall Learn; the law holdeth well.
    And that which is to be,
Ye will know at last; why weep before the hour?
  For come it shall, as out of darkness dawn.
Only may good from all this evil flower;
So prays this Heart of Argos, this frail tower
    Guarding the land alone.

> [*As they cease,* CLYTEMNESTRA *comes from the
> Palace with Attendants. She has finished her
> prayer and sacrifice, and is now wrought up
> to face the meeting with her husband. The
> Leader approaches her.*

LEADER.

Before thy state, O Queen, I bow mine eyes.
'Tis written, when the man's throne empty lies,
The woman shall be honoured.—Hast thou heard
Some tiding sure? Or is it Hope, hath stirred
To fire these altars? Dearly though we seek
To learn, 'tis thine to speak or not to speak.

CLYTEMNESTRA.

Glad-voiced, the old saw telleth, comes this morn,
The Star-child of a dancing midnight born,
And beareth to thine ear a word of joy
Beyond all hope: the Greek hath taken Troy.

LEADER.

How?
Thy word flies past me, being incredible.

CLYTEMNESTRA.

Ilion is ours.   No riddling tale I tell.

LEADER.

Such joy comes knocking at the gate of tears.

CLYTEMNESTRA.

Aye, 'tis a faithful heart that eye declares.

LEADER.

What warrant hast thou?   Is there proof of this?

CLYTEMNESTRA.

There is; unless a God hath lied there is.

LEADER.

Some dream-shape came to thee in speaking guise?

CLYTEMNESTRA.

Who deemeth me a dupe of drowsing eyes?

LEADER.

Some word within that hovereth without wings?

CLYTEMNESTRA.

Am I a child to hearken to such things?

LEADER.

Troy fallen?—But how long?   When fell she, say?

CLYTEMNESTRA.

The very night that mothered this new day.

LEADER.

And who of heralds with such fury came?

CLYTEMNESTRA.

A Fire-god, from Mount Ida scattering flame.
Whence starting, beacon after beacon burst
In flaming message hitherward. Ida first
Told Hermes' Lemnian Rock, whose answering sign
Was caught by towering Athos, the divine,
With pines immense—yea, fishes of the night
Swam skyward, drunken with that leaping light,
Which swelled like some strange sun, till dim and far
Makistos' watchmen marked a glimmering star;
They, nowise loath nor idly slumber-won,
Spring up to hurl the fiery message on,
And a far light beyond the Eurîpus tells
That word hath reached Messapion's sentinels.
They beaconed back, then onward with a high
Heap of dead heather flaming to the sky.
And onward still, not failing nor aswoon,
Across the Asôpus like a beaming moon
The great word leapt, and on Kithairon's height
Uproused a new relay of racing light.
His watchers knew the wandering flame, nor hid
Their welcome, burning higher than was bid.
Out over Lake Gorgôpis then it floats,
To Aigiplanctos, waking the wild goats,
Crying for " Fire, more Fire! " And fire was reared,
Stintless and high, a stormy streaming beard,

That waved in flame beyond the promontory
Rock-ridged, that watches the Saronian sea,
Kindling the night: then one short swoop to catch
The Spider's Crag, our city's tower of watch;
Whence hither to the Atreidae's roof it came,
A light true-fathered of Idaean flame.
Torch-bearer after torch-bearer, behold
The tale thereof in stations manifold,
Each one by each made perfect ere it passed,
And Victory in the first as in the last.
These be my proofs and tokens that my lord
From Troy hath spoke to me a burning word.

LEADER.

Woman, speak on. Hereafter shall my prayer
Be raised to God; now let me only hear,
Again and full, the marvel and the joy.

CLYTEMNESTRA.

Now, even now, the Achaian holdeth Troy!
Methinks there is a crying in her streets
That makes no concord. When sweet unguent
    meets
With vinegar in one phial, I warrant none
Shall lay those wranglers lovingly at one.
So conquerors and conquered shalt thou hear,
Two sundered tones, two lives of joy or fear.
    Here women in the dust about their slain,
Husbands or brethren, and by dead old men
Pale children who shall never more be free,
For all they loved on earth cry desolately.
And hard beside them war-stained Greeks, whom stark
Battle and then long searching through the dark

Hath gathered, ravenous, in the dawn, to feast
At last on all the plenty Troy possessed,
No portion in that feast nor ordinance,
But each man clutching at the prize of chance.
Aye, there at last under good roofs they lie
Of men spear-quelled, no frosts beneath the sky,
No watches more, no bitter moony dew. . . .
How blessèd they will sleep the whole night
    through!
Oh, if these days they keep them free from sin
Toward Ilion's conquered shrines and Them within
Who watch unconquered, maybe not again
The smiter shall be smit, the taker ta'en.
May God but grant there fall not on that host
The greed of gold that maddeneth and the lust
To spoil inviolate things! But half the race
Is run which windeth back to home and peace.
Yea, though of God they pass unchallengèd,
Methinks the wound of all those desolate dead
Might waken, groping for its will. . . .
                 Ye hear

A woman's word, belike a woman's fear.
May good but conquer in the last incline
Of the balance! Of all prayers that prayer is mine.

LEADER.

O Woman, like a man faithful and wise
Thou speakest. I accept thy testimonies
And turn to God with praising, for a gain
Is won this day that pays for all our pain.

    [CLYTEMNESTRA *returns to the Palace. The*
        CHORUS *take up their position for the Second*
        Stasimon.

An Elder.

O Zeus, All-ruler, and Night the Aid,
Gainer of glories, and hast thou thrown
'Over the towers of Ilion
   Thy net close-laid,
That none so nimble and none so tall
Shall escape withal
The snare of the slaver that claspeth all?

Another.

And Zeus the Watcher of Friend and Friend
I also praise, who hath wrought this end.
Long since on Paris his shaft he drew,
   And hath aimèd true,
Not too soon falling nor yet too far,
The fire of the avenging star.

Chorus.

*(This is God's judgement upon Troy. May it not be
   too fierce! Gold cannot save one who spurneth
   Justice.)*

The stroke of Zeus hath found them! Clear this day
   The tale, and plain to trace.
He judged, and Troy hath fallen.—And have men said
That God not deigns to mark man's hardihead,
   Trampling to earth the grace
Of holy and delicate things?—Sin lies that way.
For visibly Pride doth breed its own return
  On prideful men, who, when their houses swell
    With happy wealth, breathe ever wrath and
    blood.
Yet not too fierce let the due vengeance burn;

Only as deemeth well
    One wise of mood.

    Never shall state nor gold
      Shelter his heart from aching
    Whoso the Altar of Justice old
      Spurneth to Night unwaking.

(*The Sinner suffers in his longing till at last Tempta-*
tion overcomes him; as longing for Helen over-
came Paris.)

The tempting of misery forceth him, the dread
    Child of fore-scheming Woe!
And help is vain; the fell desire within
Is veilèd not, but shineth bright like Sin:
    And as false gold will show
Black where the touchstone trieth, so doth fade
His honour in God's ordeal. Like a child,
   Forgetting all, he hath chased his wingèd bird,
    And planted amid his people a sharp thorn.
And no God hears his prayer, or, have they heard,
   The man so base-beguiled
    They cast to scorn.

    Paris to Argos came;
      Love of a woman led him;
    So God's altar he brought to shame,
      Robbing the hand that fed him.

(*Helen's flight; the visions seen by the King's seers;*
the phantom of Helen and the King's grief.)

She hath left among her people   a noise of shield and
    sword,
  A tramp of men armèd   where the long ships are
    moored;

She hath ta'en in her goings   Desolation as a dower;
She hath stept, stept quickly,   through the great gated
    Tower,
    And the thing that could not be,   it hath been!
And the Seers they saw visions,   and they spoke of
    strange ill:
    " A Palace, a Palace;   and a great King thereof:
    A bed, a bed empty,   that was once pressed in
    love:
And thou, thou, what art thou?   Let us be, thou
    so still,
    Beyond wrath, beyond beseeching,   to the lips reft
    of thee!"
    For she whom he desireth   is beyond the deep sea,
    And a ghost in his castle   shall be queen.

        Images in sweet guise
          Carven shall move him never,
        Where is Love amid empty eyes?
          Gone, gone for ever!

*(His dreams and his suffering; but the War that he
    made caused greater and wider suffering.)*
But a shape that is a dream,   'mid the breathings of
    the night,
Cometh near, full of tears,   bringing vain vain
    delight:
For in vain when, desiring,   he can feel the joy's
    breath
—Nevermore!   Nevermore!—from   his   arms   it
    vanisheth,
    As a bird along the wind-ways of sleep.

In the mid castle hall, on the hearthstone of the
    Kings,
These griefs there be, and griefs passing these,
But in each man's dwelling of the host that sailed
    the seas,
A sad woman waits; she has thoughts of many
    things,
    And patience in her heart lieth deep.

      Knoweth she them she sent,
        Knoweth she? Lo, returning,
      Comes in stead of the man that went
        Armour and dust of burning.

(*The return of the funeral urns; the murmurs of the
    People.*)

And the gold-changer, Ares, who changeth quick
    for dead,
Who poiseth his scale in the striving of the
    spears,
Back from Troy sendeth dust, heavy dust, wet with
    tears,
Sendeth ashes with men's names in his urns neatly
    spread.
And they weep over the men, and they praise them
    one by one,
How this was a wise fighter, and this nobly
    slain—
    " Fighting to win back another's wife! "
Till a murmur is begun,
    And there steals an angry pain
      Against Kings too forward in the strife.

There by Ilion's gate
　Many a soldier sleepeth,
Young men beautiful; fast in hate
　Troy her conqueror keepeth.

(*For the Shedder of Blood is in great peril, and
not unmarked by God. May I never be a Sacker
of Cities!*)

But the rumour of the People,　it is heavy, it is chill;
And tho' no curse be spoken,　like a curse doth it
　　brood;
And my heart waits some tiding　which the dark
　　holdeth still,
For of God not unmarked　is the shedder of much
　　blood.
And who conquers beyond right　. . . Lo, the life of
　　man decays;
　There be Watchers dim his light in the wasting of
　　　the years;
　He falls, he is forgotten, and hope dies.
There is peril in the praise
　Over-praisèd that he hears;
　　For the thunder it is hurled from God's eyes.

　　Glory that breedeth strife,
　　　Pride of the Sacker of Cities;
　　Yea, and the conquered captive's life,
　　　Spare me, O God of Pities!

DIVERS ELDERS.
—The fire of good tidings it hath sped the city
　through,
　But who knows if a god mocketh? Or who knows
　　if all be true?

'Twere the fashion of a child,
Or a brain dream-beguiled,
To be kindled by the first
Torch's message as it burst,
And thereafter, as it dies, to die too.

—'Tis like a woman's sceptre, to ordain
Welcome to joy before the end is plain!

—Too lightly opened are a woman's ears;
Her fence downtrod by many trespassers,
And quickly crossed; but quickly lost
The burden of a woman's hopes or fears.

[*Here a break occurs in the action, like the descent
of the curtain in a modern theatre. A space
of some days is assumed to have passed and
we find the Elders again assembled.*

LEADER.

Soon surely shall we read the message right;
Were fire and beacon-call and lamps of light
True speakers, or but happy things that seem
And are not, like sweet voices in a dream.
I see a Herald yonder by the shore,
Shadowed with olive sprays. And from his sore
Rent raiment cries a witness from afar,
Dry Dust, born brother to the Mire of war,
That mute he comes not, neither through the smoke
Of mountain forests shall his tale be spoke;
But either shouting for a joyful day,
Or else. . . . But other thoughts I cast away.
As good hath dawned, may good shine on, we pray!

—And whoso for this City prayeth aught
Else, let him reap the harvest of his thought!

> [*Enter the* HERALD, *running. His garments are
> torn and war-stained. He falls upon his
> knees and kisses the Earth, and salutes each
> Altar in turn.*

HERALD.

Land of my fathers! Argos! Am I here . . .
Home, home at this tenth shining of the year,
And all Hope's anchors broken save this one!
For scarcely dared I dream, here in mine own
Argos at last to fold me to my rest. . . .
But now—All Hail, O Earth! O Sunlight blest!
And Zeus Most High!

> [*Checking himself as he sees the altar of Apollo.*

And thou, O Pythian Lord;
No more on us be thy swift arrows poured!
Beside Scamander well we learned how true
Thy hate is. Oh, as thou art Healer too,
Heal us! As thou art Saviour of the Lost,
Save also us, Apollo, being so tossed
With tempest! . . . All ye Daemons of the Pale!
And Hermes! Hermes, mine own guardian, hail!
Herald beloved, to whom all heralds bow. . . .
Ye Blessèd Dead that sent us, receive now
In love your children whom the spear hath spared.

O House of Kings, O roof-tree thrice-endeared,
O solemn thrones! O gods that face the sun!
Now, now, if ever in the days foregone,
After these many years, with eyes that burn,
Give hail and glory to your King's return!

For Agamemnon cometh! A great light
Cometh to men and gods out of the night.
    Grand greeting give him—aye, it need be grand—
Who, God's avenging mattock in his hand,
Hath wrecked Troy's towers and digged her soil
        beneath,
Till her gods' houses, they are things of death;
Her altars waste, and blasted every seed
Whence life might rise! So perfect is his deed,
So dire the yoke on Ilion he hath cast,
The first Atreides, King of Kings at last,
And happy among men! To whom we give
Honour most high above all things that live.
    For Paris nor his guilty land can score
The deed they wrought above the pain they bore.
"Spoiler and thief," he heard God's judgement pass;
Whereby he lost his plunder, and like grass
Mowed down his father's house and all his land;
And Troy pays twofold for the sin she planned.

LEADER.
Be glad, thou Herald of the Greek from Troy!

HERALD.
So glad, I am ready, if God will, to die!

LEADER.
Did love of this land work thee such distress?

HERALD.
The tears stand in mine eyes for happiness.

LEADER.
Sweet sorrow was it, then, that on you fell.

HERALD.

How sweet? I cannot read thy parable.

LEADER.

To pine again for them that loved you true.

HERALD.

Did ye then pine for us, as we for you?

LEADER.

The whole land's heart was dark, and groaned for
      thee.

HERALD.

Dark? For what cause? Why should such dark-
      ness be?

LEADER.

Silence in wrong is our best medicine here.

HERALD.

Your kings were gone. What others need you fear?

LEADER.

'Tis past! Like thee now, I could gladly die.

HERALD.

Even so! 'Tis past, and all is victory.
And, for our life in those long years, there were
Doubtless some grievous days, and some were fair.
Who but a god goes woundless all his way? . . .
   Oh, could I tell the sick toil of the day,
The evil nights, scant decks ill-blanketed;
The rage and cursing when our daily bread
Came not! And then on land 'twas worse than all.

Our quarters close beneath the enemy's wall;
And rain—and from the ground the river dew—
Wet, always wet! Into our clothes it grew,
Plague-like, and bred foul beasts in every hair.

 Would I could tell how ghastly midwinter
Stole down from Ida till the birds dropped dead!
Or the still heat, when on his noonday bed
The breathless blue sea sank without a wave! . . .

 Why think of it? They are past and in the grave,
All those long troubles. For I think the slain
Care little if they sleep or rise again;
And we, the living, wherefore should we ache
With counting all our lost ones, till we wake
The old malignant fortunes? If Good-bye
Comes from their side, Why, let them go, say I.
Surely for us, who live, good doth prevail
Unchallenged, with no wavering of the scale;
Wherefore we vaunt unto these shining skies,
As wide o'er sea and land our glory flies:
" By men of Argolis who conquered Troy,
These spoils, a memory and an ancient joy,
Are nailed in the gods' houses throughout Greece."
Which whoso readeth shall with praise increase
Our land, our kings, and God's grace manifold
Which made these marvels be.—My tale is told.

LEADER.

Indeed thou conquerest me. Men say, the light
In old men's eyes yet serves to learn aright.
But Clytemnestra and the House should hear
These tidings first, though I their health may share.

  [*During the last words* CLYTEMNESTRA *has entered from the Palace.*

CLYTEMNESTRA.

Long since I lifted up my voice in joy,
When the first messenger from flaming Troy
Spake through the dark of sack and overthrow.
And mockers chid me: " Because beacons show
On the hills, must Troy be fallen? Quickly born
Are women's hopes!" Aye, many did me scorn;
Yet gave I sacrifice; and by my word
Through all the city our woman's cry was
    heard,
Lifted in blessing round the seats of God,
And slumbrous incense o'er the altars glowed
In fragrance.
                And for thee, what need to tell
Thy further tale? My lord himself shall well
Instruct me. Yet, to give my lord and king
All reverent greeting at his homecoming—
What dearer dawn on woman's eyes can flame
Than this, which casteth wide her gate to acclaim
The husband whom God leadeth safe from war?—
Go, bear my lord this prayer: That fast and far
He haste him to this town which loves his name;
And in his castle may he find the same
Wife that he left, a watchdog of the hall,
True to one voice and fierce to others all;
A body and soul unchanged, no seal of his
Broke in the waiting years.—No thought of ease
Nor joy from other men hath touched my soul,
Nor shall touch, until bronze be dyed like wool.

  A boast so faithful and so plain, I wot,
Spoke by a royal Queen doth shame her not.

                    [*Exit* CLYTEMNESTRA.

LEADER.

Let thine ear mark her message. 'Tis of fair
Seeming, and craves a clear interpreter. . . .
But, Herald, I would ask thee; tell me true
Of Menelaüs. Shall he come with you,
Our land's belovèd crown, untouched of ill?

HERALD.

I know not how to speak false words of weal
For friends to reap thereof a harvest true.

LEADER.

Canst speak of truth with comfort joined? Those two
Once parted, 'tis a gulf not lightly crossed.

HERALD.

Your king is vanished from the Achaian host,
He and his ship! Such comfort have I brought.

LEADER.

Sailed he alone from Troy? Or was he caught
By storms in the midst of you, and swept away?

HERALD.

Thou hast hit the truth; good marksman, as men say!
And long to suffer is but brief to tell.

LEADER.

How ran the sailors' talk? Did there prevail
One rumour, showing him alive or dead?

HERALD.

None knoweth, none hath tiding, save the head
Of Helios, ward and watcher of the world.

LEADER.

Then tell us of the storm. How, when God hurled
His anger, did it rise? How did it die?

HERALD.

It likes me not, a day of presage high
With dolorous tongue to stain. Those twain, I vow,
Stand best apart. When one with shuddering brow,
From armies lost, back beareth to his home
Word that the terror of her prayers is come;
One wound in her great heart, and many a fate
For many a home of men cast out to sate
The two-fold scourge that worketh Ares' lust,
Spear crossed with spear, dust wed with bloody dust;
Who walketh laden with such weight of wrong,
Why, let him, if he will, uplift the song
That is Hell's triumph. But to come as I
Am now come, laden with deliverance high,
Home to a land of peace and laughing eyes,
And mar all with that fury of the skies
Which made our Greeks curse God—how should this
    be?
   Two enemies most ancient, Fire and Sea,
A sudden friendship swore, and proved their plight
By war on us poor sailors through that night
Of misery, when the horror of the wave
Towered over us, and winds from Strymon drave
Hull against hull, till good ships, by the horn
Of the mad whirlwind gored and overborne,
One here, one there, 'mid rain and blinding spray,
Like sheep by a devil herded, passed away.
And when the blessèd Sun upraised his head,
We saw the Aegean waste a-foam with dead,

Dead men, dead ships, and spars disasterful.
Howbeit for us, our one unwounded hull
Out of that wrath was stolen or begged free
By some good spirit—sure no man was he!—
Who guided clear our helm; and on till now
Hath Saviour Fortune throned her on the prow,
No surge to mar our mooring, and no floor
Of rock to tear us when we made for shore.
Till, fled from that sea-hell, with the clear sun
Above us and all trust in fortune gone,
We drove like sheep the thoughts about our brain
Of that lost army, broken and scourged amain
With evil.   And, methinks, if there is breath
In them, they talk of us as gone to death—
How else?—and so say we of them!   For thee,
Since Menelaüs thy first care must be,
If by some word of Zeus, who wills not yet
To leave the old house for ever desolate,
Some ray of sunlight on a far-off sea
Lights him, yet green and living . . . we may see
His ship some day in the harbour!—'Twas the word
Of truth ye asked me for, and truth ye have heard!

> [*Exit* HERALD.   *The* CHORUS *take position for
> the Third Stasimon.*

CHORUS.

(*Surely there was mystic meaning in the name*
    HELENA, *meaning which was fulfilled when she
    fled to Troy.*)

> Who was He   who found for thee
> That name, truthful utterly—
> Was it One beyond our vision
> Moving sure in pre-decision

Of man's doom his mystic lips?—
Calling thee, the Battle-wed,
Thee, the Strife-encompassèd,
HELEN? Yea, in fate's derision,
  Hell in cities, Hell in ships,
Hell in hearts of men they knew her,
  When the dim and delicate fold
  Of her curtains backward rolled,
And to sea, to sea, she threw her
  In the West Wind's giant hold;
And with spear and sword behind her
  Came the hunters in a flood,
Down the oarblade's viewless trail
Tracking, till in Simoïs' vale
Through the leaves they crept to find her,
  A Wrath, a seed of blood.

(*The Trojans welcomed her with triumph and praised*
Alexander, till at last their song changed and they
saw another meaning in Alexander's name also.)

So the Name to Ilion came
  On God's thought-fulfilling flame,
She a vengeance and a token
Of the unfaith to bread broken,
  Of the hearth of God betrayed,
    Against them whose voices swelled
    Glorying in the prize they held
And the Spoiler's vaunt outspoken
  And the song his brethren made
'Mid the bridal torches burning;
  Till, behold, the ancient City
Of King Priam turned, and turning
Took a new song for her learning,

A song changed and full of pity,
With the cry of a lost nation;
    And she changed the bridegroom's name:
Called him Paris Ghastly-wed;
For her sons were with the dead,
And her life one lamentation,
    'Mid blood and burning flame.

(Like a lion's whelp reared as a pet and turning after-
    wards to a great beast of prey,)

Lo, once there was a herdsman reared
    In his own house, so stories tell,
A lion's whelp, a milk-fed thing
And soft in life's first opening
Among the sucklings of the herd;
    The happy children loved him well,
And old men smiled, and oft, they say,
In men's arms, like a babe, he lay,
Bright-eyed, and toward the hand that teased him
    Eagerly fawning for food or play.

Then on a day outflashed the sudden
    Rage of the lion brood of yore;
He paid his debt to them that fed
With wrack of herds and carnage red,
Yea, wrought him a great feast unbidden,
    Till all the house-ways ran with gore;
A sight the thralls fled weeping from,
    A great red slayer, beard a-foam,
High-priest of some blood-cursèd altar
    God had uplifted against that home.

    (So was it with Helen in Troy.)

And how shall I call the thing that came
　At the first hour to Ilion city?
Call it a dream of peace untold,
A secret joy in a mist of gold,
A woman's eye that was soft, like flame,
　A flower which ate a man's heart with pity.

But she swerved aside and wrought to her kiss a
　bitter ending,
And a wrath was on her harbouring, a wrath upon
　her friending,
　When to Priam and his sons she fled quickly o'er
　　the deep,
With the god to whom she sinned for her watcher
　on the wind,
　A death-bride, whom brides long shall weep.

*(Men say that Good Fortune wakes the envy of God;
　not so; Good Fortune may be innocent, and then
　there is no vengeance.)*

A grey word liveth, from the morn
　Of old time among mortals spoken,
That man's Wealth waxen full shall fall
Not childless, but get sons withal;
And ever of great bliss is born
　A tear unstanched and a heart broken.

But I hold my thought alone and by others
　unbeguiled;
'Tis the deed that is unholy shall have issue, child on
　child,
Sin on sin, like his begetters; and they shall be as
　they were.

But the man who walketh straight, and the house
> thereof, tho' Fate
Exalt him, the children shall be fair.

(*It is Sin, it is Pride and Ruthlessness, that beget children like themselves till Justice is fulfilled upon
them.*)

But Old Sin loves, when comes the hour again,
> To bring forth New,
Which laugheth lusty amid the tears of men;
Yea, and Unruth, his comrade, wherewith none
May plead nor strive, which dareth on and on,
> Knowing not fear nor any holy thing;
Two fires of darkness in a house, born true,
> Like to their ancient spring.

But Justice shineth in a house low-wrought
> With smoke-stained wall,
And honoureth him who filleth his own lot;
But the unclean hand upon the golden stair
With eyes averse she flieth, seeking where
> Things innocent are; and, recking not the power
Of wealth by man misgloried, guideth all
> To her own destined hour.

> [*Here amid a great procession enter* AGAMEM-
> NON *on a Chariot. Behind him on another
> Chariot is* CASSANDRA. *The* CHORUS *ap-
> proach and make obeisance. Some of* AGA-
> MEMNON'S *men have on their shields a
> White Horse, some a Lion. Their arms are
> rich and partly barbaric.*

LEADER.

All hail, O King! Hail, Atreus' Son!
Sacker of Cities! Ilion's bane!

With what high word shall I greet thee again,
How give thee worship, and neither outrun
The point of pleasure, nor stint too soon?
For many will cling To fair seeming
The faster because they have sinned erewhile;
And a man may sigh with never a sting
Of grief in his heart, and a man may smile
With eyes unlit and a lip that strains.
But the wise Shepherd knoweth his sheep,
     And his eyes pierce deep
The faith like water that fawns and feigns.

But I hide nothing, O King. That day
When in quest of Helen our battle array
Hurled forth, thy name upon my heart's scroll
Was deep in letters of discord writ;
     And the ship of thy soul,
Ill-helmed and blindly steered was it,
Pursuing ever, through men that die,
One wild heart that was fain to fly.
     But on this new day,
From the deep of my thought and in love, I
     say
 " Sweet is a grief well ended; "
And in time's flow Thou wilt learn and know
     The true from the false,
Of them that were left to guard the walls
     Of thine empty Hall unfriended.

[*During the above* CLYTEMNESTRA *has appeared
on the Palace steps, with a train of Attendants, to receive her Husband.*

AGAMEMNON

To Argos and the gods of Argolis
All hail, who share with me the glory of this
Home-coming and the vengeance I did wreak
On Priam's City!   Yea, though none should speak,
The great gods heard our cause, and in one mood
Uprising, in the urn of bitter blood,
That men should shriek and die and towers should
       burn,
Cast their great vote; while over Mercy's urn
Hope waved her empty hands and nothing fell.

   Even now in smoke that City tells her tale;
The wrack-wind liveth, and where Ilion died
The reek of the old fatness of her pride
From hot and writhing ashes rolls afar.

       For which let thanks, wide as our glories are,
Be uplifted; seeing the Beast of Argos hath
Round Ilion's towers piled high his fence of wrath
And, for one woman ravished, wrecked by force
A City.   Lo, the leap of the wild Horse
In darkness when the Pleiades were dead;
A mailèd multitude, a Lion unfed,
Which leapt the tower and lapt the blood of Kings!

   Lo, to the Gods I make these thanksgivings.
But for thy words: I marked them, and I mind
Their meaning, and my voice shall be behind
Thine.   For not many men, the proverb saith,
Can love a friend whom fortune prospereth
Unenvying; and about the envious brain
Cold poison clings, and doubles all the pain
Life brings him.   His own woundings he must nurse,
And feels another's gladness like a curse.

Well can I speak. I know the mirrored glass
Called friendship, and the shadow shapes that pass
And feign them a King's friends. I have known but
    one—
Odysseus, him we trapped against his own
Will!—who once harnessed bore his yoke right
    well . . .
Be he alive or dead of whom I tell
The tale. And for the rest, touching our state
And gods, we will assemble in debate
A concourse of all Argos, taking sure
Counsel, that what is well now may endure
Well, and if aught needs healing medicine, still
By cutting and by fire, with all good will,
I will essay to avert the after-wrack
Such sickness breeds.

                        Aye, Heaven hath led me back;
And on this hearth where still my fire doth burn
I will go pay to heaven my due return,
Which guides me here, which saved me far away.
    O Victory, now mine own, be mine alway!

> [CLYTEMNESTRA, *at the head of her retinue, steps
> forward. She controls her suspense with
> difficulty but gradually gains courage as she
> proceeds.*

CLYTEMNESTRA.

Ye Elders, Council of the Argive name
Here present, I will no more hold it shame
To lay my passion bare before men's eyes.
There comes a time to a woman when fear dies
For ever. None hath taught me. None could tell,
Save me, the weight of years intolerable

I lived while this man lay at Ilion.
That any woman thus should sit alone
In a half-empty house, with no man near,
Makes her half-blind with dread! And in her ear
Alway some voice of wrath; now messengers
Of evil; now not so; then others worse,
Crying calamity against mine and me.

  Oh, had he half the wounds that variously
Came rumoured home, his flesh must be a net,
All holes from heel to crown! And if he met
As many deaths as I met tales thereon,
Is he some monstrous thing, some Gêryon
Three-souled, that will not die, till o'er his head,
Three robes of earth be piled, to hold him dead?

  Aye, many a time my heart broke, and the noose
Of death had got me; but they cut me loose.
It was those voices alway in mine ear.

  For that, too, young Orestes is not here
Beside me, as were meet, seeing he above
All else doth hold the surety of our love;
Let not thy heart be troubled. It fell thus:
Our loving spear-friend took him, Strophius
The Phocian, who forewarned me of annoy
Two-fronted, thine own peril under Troy,
And ours here, if the rebel multitude
Should cast the Council down. It is men's mood
Alway, to spurn the fallen. So spake he,
And sure no guile was in him.
                              But for me,
The old stormy rivers of my grief are dead
Now at the spring; not one tear left unshed.
Mine eyes are sick with vigil, endlessly

Weeping the beacon-piles that watched for thee
For ever answerless. And did I dream,
A gnat's thin whirr would start me, like a scream
Of battle, and show me thee by terrors swept,
Crowding, too many for the time I slept.

From all which stress delivered and free-souled,
I greet my lord: O watchdog of the fold,
O forestay sure that fails not in the squall,
O strong-based pillar of a towering hall;
O single son to a father age-ridden;
O land unhoped for seen by shipwrecked men;
Sunshine more beautiful when storms are fled;
Spring of quick water in a desert dead. . . .
How sweet to be set free from any chain!

These be my words to greet him home again.
No god shall grudge them. Surely I and thou
Have suffered in time past enough! And now
Dismount, O head with love and glory crowned,
From this high car; yet plant not on bare ground
Thy foot, great King, the foot that trampled Troy.
Ho, bondmaids, up! Forget not your employ,
A floor of crimson broideries to spread
For the King's path. Let all the ground be red
Where those feet pass; and Justice, dark of yore,
Home light him to the hearth he looks not for!
What followeth next, our sleepless care shall see
Ordered as God's good pleasure may decree.

[*The attendants spread tapestries of crimson and
gold from the Chariot to the Door of the
Palace.* AGAMEMNON *does not move.*

AGAMEMNON.

Daughter of Leda, watcher of my fold,
In sooth thy welcome, grave and amply told,
Fitteth mine absent years. Though it had been
Seemlier, methinks, some other, not my Queen,
Had spoke these honours. For the rest, I say,
Seek not to make me soft in woman's way;
Cry not thy praise to me wide-mouthed, nor fling
Thy body down, as to some barbarous king.
Nor yet with broidered hangings strew my path,
To awake the unseen ire. 'Tis God that hath
Such worship; and for mortal man to press
Rude feet upon this broidered loveliness . . .
I vow there is danger in it. Let my road
Be honoured, surely; but as man, not god.
Rugs for the feet and yonder broidered pall . . .
The names ring diverse! . . . Aye, and not to fall
Suddenly blind is of all gifts the best
God giveth, for I reckon no man blest
Ere to the utmost goal his race be run.
    So be it; and if, as this day I have done,
I shall do always, then I fear no ill.

CLYTEMNESTRA.
Tell me but this, nowise against thy will . . .

AGAMEMNON.
My will, be sure, shall falter not nor fade.

CLYTEMNESTRA.
Was this a vow in some great peril made?

AGAMEMNON.
Enough! I have spoke my purpose, fixed and plain.

CLYTEMNESTRA.

Were Priam the conqueror . . . Think, would he refrain?

AGAMEMNON.

Oh, stores of broideries would be trampled then!

CLYTEMNESTRA.

Lord, care not for the cavillings of men!

AGAMEMNON.

The murmur of a people hath strange weight.

CLYTEMNESTRA.

Who feareth envy, feareth to be great.

AGAMEMNON.

'Tis graceless when a woman strives to lead.

CLYTEMNESTRA.

When a great conqueror yields, 'tis grace indeed.

AGAMEMNON.

So in this war thou must my conqueror be?

CLYTEMNESTRA.

Yield! With good will to yield is victory!

AGAMEMNON.

Well, if I needs must . . . Be it as thou hast said!
. Quick! Loose me these bound slaves on which I tread,

And while I walk yon wonders of the sea
God grant no eye of wrath be cast on me
From far!

> [*The Attendants untie his shoes.*

For even now it likes me not
To waste mine house, thus marring underfoot
The pride thereof, and wondrous broideries
Bought in far seas with silver. But of these
Enough.—And mark, I charge thee, this princess
Of Ilion; tend her with all gentleness.
God's eye doth see, and loveth from afar,
The merciful conqueror. For no slave of war
Is slave by his own will. She is the prize
And chosen flower of Ilion's treasuries,
Set by the soldiers' gift to follow me.

Now therefore, seeing I am constrained by thee
And do thy will, I walk in conqueror's guise
Beneath my Gate, trampling sea-crimson dyes.

> [*As he dismounts and sets foot on the Tapestries*
> CLYTEMNESTRA'S *women utter again their*
> *Cry of Triumph. The people bow or kneel*
> *as he passes.*

CLYTEMNESTRA.

There is the sea—its caverns who shall drain?
Breeding of many a purple-fish the stain
Surpassing silver, ever fresh renewed,
For robes of kings. And we, by right indued,
Possess our fill thereof. Thy house, O King,
Knoweth no stint, nor lack of anything.

What trampling of rich raiment, had the cry
So sounded in the domes of prophesy,

Would I have vowed these years, as price to pay
For this dear life in peril far away!
Where the root is, the leafage cometh soon
To clothe an house, and spread its leafy boon
Against the burning star; and, thou being come,
Thou, on the midmost hearthstone of thy home,
Oh, warmth in winter leapeth to thy sign.
And when God's summer melteth into wine
The green grape, on that house shall coolness fall
Where the true man, the master, walks his hall.

Zeus, Zeus! True Master, let my prayers be true!
And, oh, forget not that thou art willed to do!

> [*She follows* AGAMEMNON *into the Palace. The
> retinues of both King and Queen go in after
> them.* CASSANDRA *remains.*

CHORUS.
What is this that evermore,   [*Strophe* 1.
A cold terror at the door
Of this bosom presage-haunted,
Pale as death   hovereth?
While a song unhired, unwanted,
By some inward prophet chanted,
Speaks the secret at its core;
And to cast it from my blood
Like a dream not understood
No sweet-spoken Courage now
Sitteth at my heart's dear prow.

Yet I know that manifold
Days, like sand, have waxen old

Since the day those shoreward-thrown
　　Cables flapped and line on line
Standing forth for Ilion
　　The long galleys took the brine.

　　　　　　　　　　　　　　　[*Antistrophe* 1.

And in harbour—mine own eye
Hath beheld—again they lie;
Yet that lyreless music hid'.en
　　Whispers still words of ill,
'Tis the Soul of me unbidden,
Like some Fury sorrow-ridden,
　　Weeping over things that die.
　　Neither waketh in my sense
　　Ever Hope's dear confidence;
　　For this flesh that groans within,
　　And these bones that know of Sin,
　　This tossed heart upon the spate
　　Of a whirpool that is Fate,
　　Surely these lie not. Yet deep
　　　　Beneath hope my prayer doth run,
　　All will die like dreams, and creep
　　　　To the unthought of and undone.

　　　　　　　　　　　　　　　　[*Strophe* 2.

—Surely of great Weal at the end of all
Comes not Content; so near doth Fever crawl,
Close neighbour, pressing hard the narrow wall.

—Woe to him who fears not fate!
　　'Tis the ship that forward straight
　　Sweepeth, strikes the reef below;
　　He who fears and lightens weight,

Casting forth, in measured throw,
From the wealth his hand hath got . . .
His whole ship shall founder not,
With abundance overfraught,
Nor deep seas above him flow.
—Lo, when famine stalketh near,
One good gift of Zeus again
From the furrows of one year
Endeth quick the starving pain;

[*Antistrophe* 2.

—But once the blood of death is fallen, black
And oozing at a slain man's feet, alack!
By spell or singing who shall charm it back?

—One there was of old who showed
Man the path from death to day;
But Zeus, lifting up his rod,
Spared not, when he charged him stay.

—Save that every doom of God
Hath by other dooms its way
Crossed, that none may rule alone,
In one speech-outstripping flood
Forth had all this passion flown,
Which now murmuring hides away,
Full of pain, and hoping not
Ever one clear thread to unknot
From the tangle of my soul,
From a heart of burning coal.

[*Suddenly* CLYTEMNESTRA *appears
standing in the Doorway.*

CLYTEMNESTRA.

Thou likewise, come within! I speak thy name,
Cassandra;

> [CASSANDRA *trembles, but continues to stare in
> front of her, as though not hearing* CLYTEM-
> NESTRA.

seeing the Gods—why chafe at them?—
Have placed thee here, to share within these walls
Our lustral waters, 'mid a crowd of thralls
Who stand obedient round the altar-stone
Of our Possession. Therefore come thou down,
And be not over-proud. The tale is told
How once Alcmêna's son himself, being sold,
Was patient, though he liked not the slaves' mess.

And more, if Fate must bring thee to this stress,
Praise God thou art come to a House of high report
And wealth from long ago. The baser sort,
Who have reaped some sudden harvest unforeseen,
Are ever cruel to their slaves, and mean
In the measure. We shall give whate'er is due.

> [CASSANDRA *is silent.*

LEADER.

To thee she speaks, and waits . . . clear words and
     true!
Oh, doom is all around thee like a net;
Yield, if thou canst. . . . Belike thou canst not yet,

CLYTEMNESTRA.

Methinks, unless this wandering maid is one
Voiced like a swallow-bird, with tongue unknown
And barbarous, she can read my plain intent.
I use but words, and ask for her consent.

LEADER.

Ah, come! 'Tis best, as the world lies to-day.
Leave this high-thronèd chariot, and obey!

CLYTEMNESTRA.

How long must I stand dallying at the Gate?
Even now the beasts to Hestia consecrate
Wait by the midmost fire, since there is wrought
This high fulfilment for which no man thought.
Wherefore, if 'tis thy pleasure to obey
Aught of my will, prithee, no more delay!
If, deaf to sense, thou wilt not understand . . .
Thou show her, not with speech but with brute hand!

[*To the Leader of the* CHORUS.

LEADER.

The strange maid needs a rare interpreter.
She is trembling like a wild beast in a snare.

CLYTEMNESTRA.

'Fore God, she is mad, and heareth but her own
Folly! A slave, her city all o'erthrown,
She needs must chafe her bridle, till this fret
Be foamed away in blood and bitter sweat.
  I waste no more speech, thus to be defied.

[*She goes back inside the Palace.*

LEADER.

I pity thee so sore, no wrath nor pride
Is in me.—Come, dismount! Bend to the stroke
Fate lays on thee, and learn to feel thy yoke.

[*He lays his hand softly on* CASSANDRA's *shoulder.*

CASSANDRA (*moaning to herself*).

Otototoi . . . Dreams. Dreams.
Apollo. O Apollo!

SECOND ELDER.

Why sob'st thou for Apollo? It is writ,
He loves not grief nor lendeth ear to it.

CASSANDRA.

Otototoi . . . Dreams. Dreams.
Apollo. O Apollo!

LEADER.

Still to that god she makes her sobbing cry
Who hath no place where men are sad, or die.

CASSANDRA.

Apollo, Apollo! Light of the Ways of Men!
Mine enemy!
Hast lighted me to darkness yet again?

SECOND ELDER.

How? Will she prophesy about her own
Sorrows? That power abides when all is gone!

CASSANDRA.

Apollo, Apollo! Light of all that is!
Mine enemy!
Where hast thou led me? . . . Ha! What house
is this?

LEADER.

The Atreidae's castle. If thou knowest not, I
Am here to help thee, and help faithfully.

CASSANDRA.
(*whispering*).
Nay, nay. This is the house that God hateth.
  There be many things that know its secret;
    sore
And evil things; murders and strangling death.
  'Tis here they slaughter men . . . A splashing
  floor.

SECOND ELDER.
Keen-sensed the strange maid seemeth, like a hound
For blood.—And what she seeks can sure be found!

CASSANDRA.
The witnesses . . . I follow where they lead.
  That weeping: here quite close: children are
    there,
  Weeping: and wounds that bleed.
The smell of the baked meats their father tare.

SECOND ELDER.
(*recognizing her vision, and repelled*).
Word of thy mystic power had reached our ear
Long since. Howbeit we need no prophets here.

CASSANDRA.
Ah, ah! What would they? A new dreadful thing.
  A great great sin plots in the house this day;
Too strong for the faithful, beyond medicining . . .
  And help stands far away.

LEADER.
This warning I can read not, though I knew
That other tale. It rings the city through.

CASSANDRA.

O Woman, thou! The lord who lay with thee!
  Wilt lave with water, and then . . . How speak
    the end?
It comes so quick. A hand . . . another hand . . .
  That reach, reach gropingly . . .

LEADER.

I see not yet. These riddles, pierced with blind
Gleams of foreboding but bemuse my mind.

CASSANDRA.

Ah, ah! What is it? There; it is coming clear.
  A net . . . some net of Hell.
Nay, she that lies with him . . . is she the snare?
  And half of his blood upon it. It holds well . . .
O Crowd of ravening Voices, be glad, yea, shout
And cry for the stoning, cry for the casting out!

SECOND ELDER.

What Fury Voices call'st thou to be hot
Against this castle? Such words like me not.

  And deep within my breast I felt that sick
    And saffron drop, which creepeth to the heart
    To die as the last rays of life depart.
      Misfortune comes so quick.

CASSANDRA.

Ah, look! Look! Keep his mate from the Wild
    Bull!
  A tangle of raiment, see;
A black horn, and a blow, and he falleth, full
  In the marble amid the water. I counsel ye.
  I speak plain. . . . Blood in the bath and treachery!

LEADER.

No great interpreter of oracles
Am I; but this, I think, some mischief spells.

> What spring of good hath seercraft ever made
>   Up from the dark to flow?
> 'Tis but a weaving of words, a craft of woe,
>   To make mankind afraid.

CASSANDRA.

Poor woman! Poor dead woman! . . . Yea, it is I,
    Poured out like water among them. Weep for
        me. . . .
    Ah! What is this place? Why must I come
        with thee . . .
    To die, only to die?

LEADER.

Thou art borne on the breath of God, thou spirit
    wild,
    For thine own weird to wail,
Like to that wingèd voice, that heart so sore
Which, crying alway, hungereth to cry more,
" Itylus, Itylus," till it sing her child
    Back to the nightingale.

CASSANDRA.

Oh, happy Singing Bird, so sweet, so clear!
    Soft wings for her God made,
And an easy passing, without pain or tear . . .
For me 'twill be torn flesh and rending blade.

SECOND ELDER.

Whence is it sprung, whence wafted on God's breath,
    This anguish reasonless?
This throbbing of terror shaped to melody,
Moaning of evil blent with music high?
Who hath marked out for thee that mystic path
    Through thy woe's wilderness?

CASSANDRA.

Alas for the kiss, the kiss of Paris, his people's bane!
Alas for Scamander Water, the water my fathers
    drank!
Long, long ago, I played about thy bank,
    And was cherished and grew strong;
Now by a River of Wailing, by shores of Pain,
    Soon shall I make my song.

LEADER.

How sayst thou? All too clear,
This ill word thou hast laid upon thy mouth!
    A babe could read thee plain.
It stabs within me like a serpent's tooth,
The bitter thrilling music of her pain:
    I marvel as I hear.

CASSANDRA.

Alas for the toil, the toil of a City, worn unto death!
Alas for my father's worship before the citadel,
The flocks that bled and the tumult of their breath!
    But no help from them came
To save Troy Towers from falling as they fell! . . .
And I on the earth shall writhe, my heart aflame.

SECOND ELDER.

Dark upon dark, new ominous words of ill!
 Sure there hath swept on thee some Evil Thing,
   Crushing, which makes thee bleed
 And in the torment of thy vision sing
These plaining death-fraught oracles . . . Yet still,
   still,
   Their end I cannot read!

CASSANDRA.

[*By an effort she regains mastery of herself, and
  speaks directly to the Leader.*

'Fore God, mine oracle shall no more hide
With veils his visage, like a new-wed bride!
A shining wind out of this dark shall blow,
Piercing the dawn, growing as great waves grow,
To burst in the heart of sunrise . . . stronger far
Than this poor pain of mine. I will not mar
With mists my wisdom.
                    Be near me as I go,
Tracking the evil things of long ago,
And bear me witness. For this roof, there clings
Music about it, like a choir which sings
One-voiced, but not well-sounding, for not good
The words are. Drunken, drunken, and with
   blood,
To make them dare the more, a revelling rout
Is in the rooms, which no man shall cast out,
Of sister Furies. And they weave to song,
Haunting the House, its first blind deed of wrong,
Spurning in turn that King's bed desecrate,
Defiled, which paid a brother's sin with hate. . . .

   Hath it missed or struck, mine arrow? Am I a
     poor
Dreamer, that begs and babbles at the door?
Give first thine oath in witness, that I know
Of this great dome the sins wrought long ago.

ELDER.

And how should oath of mine, though bravely sworn,
Appease thee? Yet I marvel that one born
Far over seas, of alien speech, should fall
So apt, as though she had lived here and seen all.

CASSANDRA.

The Seer Apollo made me too to see.

ELDER (*in a low voice*).

Was the God's heart pierced with desire for thee?

CASSANDRA.

Time was, I held it shame hereof to speak.

ELDER.

Ah, shame is for the mighty, not the weak.

CASSANDRA.

We wrestled, and his breath to me was sweet.

ELDER.

Ye came to the getting of children, as is meet?

CASSANDRA.

I swore to Loxias, and I swore a lie.

ELDER.

Already thine the gift of prophecy?

CASSANDRA.

Already I showed my people all their path.

ELDER.

And Loxias did not smite thee in his wrath?

CASSANDRA.

After that sin . . . no man believed me more.

ELDER.

Nay, then, to us thy wisdom seemeth sure.

CASSANDRA.

Oh, oh! Agony, agony!
Again the awful pains of prophecy
Are on me, maddening as they fall. . . .
Ye see them there . . . beating against the wall?
So young . . . like shapes that gather in a dream . . .
Slain by a hand they loved. Children they seem,
Murdered . . . and in their hands they bear baked
    meat:
I think it is themselves. Yea, flesh; I see it;
And inward parts. . . . Oh, what a horrible load
To carry! And their father drank their blood.
  From these, I warn ye, vengeance broodeth still,
A lion's rage, which goes not forth to kill
But lurketh in his lair, watching the high
Hall of my war-gone master . . . Master? Aye;
Mine, mine! The yoke is nailed about my neck. . . .
Oh, lord of ships and trampler on the wreck
Of Ilion, knows he not this she-wolf's tongue,
Which licks and fawns, and laughs with ear up-sprung,

To bite in the end like a secret death?—And can
The woman? Slay a strong and armèd man? . . .
   What fangèd reptile like to her doth creep?
Some serpent amphisbene, some Skylla, deep
Housed in the rock, where sailors shriek and die,
Mother of Hell blood-raging, which doth cry
On her own flesh war, war without alloy . . .
God! And she shouted in his face her joy,
Like men in battle when the foe doth break.
And feigns thanksgiving for his safety's sake!
   What if no man believe me? 'Tis all one.
The thing which must be shall be; aye, and soon
Thou too shalt sorrow for these things, and here
Standing confess me all too true a seer.

LEADER.

The Thyestean feast of children slain
I understood, and tremble. Aye, my brain
Reels at these visions, beyond guesswork true.
But after, though I heard, I had lost the clue.

CASSANDRA.

Man, thou shalt look on Agamemnon dead.

LEADER.

Peace, Mouth of Evil! Be those words unsaid!

CASSANDRA.

No god of peace hath watch upon that hour.

LEADER.

If it must come. Forefend it, Heavenly Power!

CASSANDRA.

They do not think of prayer; they think of death.

LEADER.

They? Say, what man this foul deed compasseth?

CASSANDRA.

Alas, thou art indeed fallen far astray!

LEADER.

How could such deed be done? I see no way.

CASSANDRA.

Yet know I not the Greek tongue all too well?

LEADER.

Greek are the Delphic dooms, but hard to spell.

CASSANDRA.

Ah! Ah! There!
What a strange fire! It moves . . . It comes at me.
O Wolf Apollo, mercy! O agony! . . .
Why lies she with a wolf, this lioness lone,
Two-handed, when the royal lion is gone?
God, she will kill me! Like to them that brew
Poison, I see her mingle for me too
A separate vial in her wrath, and swear,
Whetting her blade for him, that I must share
His death . . . because, because he hath dragged me
     here!
   Oh, why these mockers at my throat? This gear
Of wreathèd bands, this staff of prophecy?
I mean to kill you first, before I die.
Begone!

> [*She tears off her prophetic habiliments; and pres-*
>   *ently throws them on the ground, and stamps*
>   *on them.*

      Down to perdition! . . . Lie ye so?
So I requite you!   Now make rich in woe
Some other Bird of Evil, me no more!

                           [Coming to herself.

Ah, see!   It is Apollo's self, hath tore
His crown from me!   Who watched me long ago
In this same prophet's robe, by friend, by foe,
All with one voice, all blinded, mocked to scorn:
" A thing of dreams," " a beggar-maid outworn,"
Poor, starving and reviled, I endured all;
And now the Seer, who called me till my call
Was perfect, leads me to this last dismay. . . .
'Tis not the altar-stone where men did slay
My father; 'tis a block, a block with gore
Yet hot, that waits me, of one slain before.
    Yet not of God unheeded shall we lie.
There cometh after, one who lifteth high
The downfallen; a branch where blossometh
A sire's avenging and a mother's death.
Exiled and wandering, from this land outcast,
One day He shall return, and set the last
Crown on these sins that have his house downtrod.
For, lo, there is a great oath sworn of God,
His father's upturned face shall guide him home.
    Why should I grieve?   Why pity these men's doom?
I who have seen the City of Ilion
Pass as she passed; and they who cast her down
Have thus their end, as God gives judgement sure. . . .
    I go to drink my cup.   I will endure
To die.   O Gates, Death-Gates, all hail to you!
Only, pray God the blow be stricken true!
Pray God, unagonized, with blood that flows
Quick unto friendly death, these eyes may close!

LEADER.

O full of sorrows, full of wisdom great,
Woman, thy speech is a long anguish; yet,
Knowing thy doom, why walkst thou with clear eyes,
Like some god-blinded beast, to sacrifice?

CASSANDRA.

There is no escape, friends; only vain delay.

LEADER.

Is not the later still the sweeter day?

CASSANDRA.

The day is come. Small profit now to fly.

LEADER.

Through all thy griefs, Woman, thy heart is high.

CASSANDRA.

Alas! None that is happy hears that praise.

LEADER.

Are not the brave dead blest in after days?

CASSANDRA.

O Father! O my brethren brave, I come!
  [*She moves towards the House, but recoils shuddering.*

LEADER.

What frights thee? What is that thou startest from?

CASSANDRA.

Ah, faugh! Faugh!

LEADER.

What turns thee in that blind
Horror? Unless some loathing of the mind . . .

CASSANDRA.

Death drifting from the doors, and blood like rain!

LEADER.

'Tis but the dumb beasts at the altar slain.

CASSANDRA.

And vapours from a charnel-house . . . See there!

LEADER.

'Tis Tyrian incense clouding in the air.

CASSANDRA (*recovering herself again*).

So be it!—I will go, in yonder room
To weep mine own and Agamemnon's doom.
May death be all! Strangers, I am no bird
That pipeth trembling at a thicket stirred
By the empty wind. Bear witness on that day
When woman for this woman's life shall pay,
And man for man ill-mated low shall lie:
I ask this boon, as being about to die.

LEADER.

Alas, I pity thee thy mystic fate!

CASSANDRA.

One word, one dirge-song would I utter yet
O'er mine own corpse. To this last shining Sun
I pray that, when the Avenger's work is done,
His enemies may remember this thing too,
This little thing, the woman slave they slew!

O world of men, farewell! A painted show
Is all thy glory; and when life is low
The touch of a wet sponge out-blotteth all.
Oh, sadder this than any proud man's fall!

> [*She goes into the House.*

CHORUS.

Great Fortune is an hungry thing,
　And filleth no heart anywhere,
Though men with fingers menacing
　Point at the great house, none will dare,
When Fortune knocks, to bar the door
Proclaiming: "Come thou here no more!"
Lo, to this man the Gods have given
　Great Ilion in the dust to tread
And home return, emblazed of heaven;
If it is writ, he too shall go
Through blood for blood spilt long ago;
If he too, dying for the dead,
　Should crown the deaths of alien years,
　What mortal afar off, who hears,
Shall boast him Fortune's Child, and led
　Above the eternal tide of tears?

> [*A sudden Cry from within.*

VOICE.

Ho! Treason in the house! I am wounded: slain.

LEADER.

Hush! In the castle! 'Twas a cry
Of some man wounded mortally.

VOICE.

Ah God, another! I am stricken again.

LEADER.

I think the deed is done. It was the King
Who groaned. . . . Stand close, and think if any-
    thing . . .

> [*The Old Men gather together under the shock,
> and debate confusedly.*

ELDER B.

I give you straight my judgement. Summon all
The citizens to rescue. Sound a call!

ELDER C.

No, no! Burst in at once without a word!
In, and convict them by their dripping sword!

ELDER D.

Yes; that or something like it. Quick, I say,
Be doing! 'Tis a time for no delay.

ELDER E.

We have time to think. This opening . . . They
    have planned
Some scheme to make enslavement of the land.

ELDER F.

Yes, while we linger here! They take no thought
Of lingering, and their sword-arm sleepeth not!

ELDER G.

I have no counsel. I can speak not. Oh,
Let him give counsel who can strike a blow!

Elder H.

I say as this man says. I have no trust
In words to raise a dead man from the dust.

Elder I.

How mean you?   Drag out our poor lives, and
    stand
Cowering to these defilers of the land?

Elder J.

Nay, 'tis too much! Better to strive and die!
Death is an easier doom than slavery.

Elder K.

We heard a sound of groaning, nothing plain,
How know we—are we seers?—that one is slain?

Elder L.

Oh, let us find the truth out, ere we grow   /
Thus passionate! To surmise is not to know.

Leader.

Break in, then! 'Tis the counsel ye all bring,
And learn for sure, how is it with the King.

> [*They cluster up towards the Palace Door, as
> though to force an entrance, when the great
> Door swings open, revealing* Clytemnestra,
> *who stands, axe in hand, over the dead bodies
> of* Agamemnon *and* Cassandra. *The body
> of* Agamemnon *is wrapped in a rich crim-
> son web. There is blood on* Clytemnes-
> tra's *brow, and she speaks in wild triumph.*

CLYTEMNESTRA.

Oh, lies enough and more have I this day
Spoken, which now I shame not to unsay.
How should a woman work, to the utter end,
Hate on a damnèd hater, feigned a friend;
How pile perdition round him, hunter-wise,
Too high for overleaping, save by lies?
To me this hour was dreamed of long ago;
A thing of ancient hate. 'Twas very slow
In coming, but it came. And here I stand
Even where I struck, with all the deed I planned
Done! 'Twas so wrought—what boots it to
  deny?—
The man could neither guard himself nor fly.
An endless web, as by some fisher strung,
A deadly plenteousness of robe, I flung
All round him, and struck twice; and with two
  cries
His limbs turned water and broke; and as he lies
I cast my third stroke in, a prayer well-sped
To Zeus of Hell, who guardeth safe his dead!
So there he gasped his life out as he lay;
And, gasping, the blood spouted . . . Like dark spray
That splashed, it came, a salt and deathly dew;
Sweet, sweet as God's dear rain-drops ever blew
O'er a parched field, the day the buds are born! . . .
 Which things being so, ye Councillors high-born,
Depart in joy, if joy ye will. For me,
I glory. Oh, if such a thing might be
As o'er the dead thank-offering to outpour,
On this dead it were just, aye, just and more,
Who filled the cup of the House with treacheries
Curse-fraught, and here hath drunk it to the lees!

LEADER.

We are astonied at thy speech. To fling,
Wild mouth! such vaunt over thy murdered King!

CLYTEMNESTRA.

Wouldst fright me, like a witless woman? Lo,
This   bosom   shakes   not.   And,   though   well   ye
    know,
I tell you . . . Curse me as ye will, or bless,
'Tis all one . . . This is Agamemnon; this,
My husband, dead by my right hand, a blow
Struck by a righteous craftsman. Aye, 'tis so.

CHORUS.

Woman, what evil tree,
    What poison grown of the ground
Or draught of the drifting sea
    Way to thy lips hath found,
Making thee clothe thy heart
    In rage, yea, in curses burning
When thine own people pray?
Thou hast hewn, thou hast cast away;
And a thing cast away thou art,
    A thing of hate and a spurning!

CLYTEMNESTRA.

Aye, now, for me, thou hast thy words of fate;
Exile from Argos and the people's hate
For ever! Against him no word was cried,
When, recking not, as 'twere a beast that died,
With flocks abounding o'er his wide domain,
He slew his child, my love, my flower of pain, . . .

Great God, as magic for the winds of Thrace!
Why was not he man-hunted from his place,
To purge the blood that stained him? . . . When
    the deed
Is mine, oh, then thou art a judge indeed!
But threat thy fill. I am ready, and I stand
Content; if thy hand beateth down my hand,
Thou rulest. If aught else be God's decree,
Thy lesson shall be learned, though late it be.

CHORUS.

    Thy thought, it is very proud;
      Thy breath is the scorner's breath;
    Is not the madness loud
      In thy heart, being drunk with death?
    Yea, and above thy brow
      A star of the wet blood burneth!
    Oh, doom shall have yet her day,
    The last friend cast away,
    When lie doth answer lie
      And a stab for a stab returneth!

CLYTEMNESTRA.

And heark what Oath-gods gather to my side!
By my dead child's Revenge, now satisfied,
By Mortal Blindness, by all Powers of Hell
Which Hate, to whom in sacrifice he fell,
My Hope shall walk not in the house of Fear,
While on my hearth one fire yet burneth clear,
One lover, one Aigisthos, as of old!
    What should I fear, when fallen here I hold
This foe, this scorner of his wife, this toy
And fool of each Chryseïs under Troy;

And there withal his soothsayer and slave,
His chanting bed-fellow, his leman brave,
Who rubbed the galleys' benches at his side?
But, oh, they had their guerdon as they died!
For he lies thus, and she, the wild swan's way,
Hath trod her last long weeping roundelay,
And lies, his lover, ravisht o'er the main
For his bed's comfort and my deep disdain.

CHORUS.

(*Some Elders.*)

Would God that suddenly
With no great agony,
   No long sick-watch to keep,
My hour would come to me,
My hour, and presently
Bring the eternal, the
   Unwaking sleep,
Now that my Shepherd, he
Whose love watched over me,
   Lies in the deep!

ANOTHER.

For woman's sake he endured and battled well,
   And by a woman's hand he fell.

OTHERS.

What hast thou done, O Helen blind of brain,
O face that slew the souls on Ilion's plain,
One face, one face, and many a thousand
   slain?

The hate of old that on this castle lay,
Builded in lust, a husband's evil day,
Hath bloomed for thee a perfect flower again
And unforgotten, an old and burning stain
    Never to pass away.

CLYTEMNESTRA.

Nay, pray not for the hour of death, being tried
    Too sore beneath these blows
Neither on Helen turn thy wrath aside,
The Slayer of Men, the face which hath destroyed
Its thousand Danaan souls, and wrought a wide
    Wound that no leech can close.

CHORUS.

—Daemon, whose heel is set
    On the House and the twofold kin
    Of the high Tantalidae,
A power, heavy as fate,
    Thou wieldest through woman's sin,
        Piercing the heart of me!

—Like a raven swoln with hate
    He hath set on the dead his claw,
He croaketh a song to sate
    His fury, and calls it Law!

CLYTEMNESTRA.

Ah, call upon Him! Yea, call—
    And thy thought hath found its path—
The Daemon who haunts this hall,
    The thrice-engorgèd Wrath;

From him is the ache of the flesh
　　For blood born and increased;
　　Ere the old sore hath ceased
　　　It oozeth afresh.

CHORUS.

—Indeed He is very great,
　　And heavy his anger, He,
　　The Daemon who guides the fate
　　Of the old Tantalidae:
Alas, alas, an evil tale ye tell
Of desolate angers and insatiable!

—Ah me,
　　And yet 'tis all as Zeus hath willed,
　　　Doer of all and Cause of all;
　　By His Word every chance doth fall,
　　　No end without Him is fulfilled;
　　　What of these things
　　But cometh by high Heaven's counsellings?

　　　　[*A band of Mourners has gathered
　　　　within the House.*

MOURNERS.

Ah, sorrow, sorrow! My King, my King!
　　How shall I weep, what word shall I say?
Caught in the web of this spider thing,
　　In foul death gasping thy life away!
Woe's me, woe's me, for this slavish lying,
The doom of craft and the lonely dying,
　　The iron two-edged and the hands that
　　　slay!

CLYTEMNESTRA.

And criest thou still this deed hath been
My work? Nay, gaze, and have no thought
That this is Agamemnon's Queen.
'Tis He, 'tis He, hath round him wrought
This phantom of the dead man's wife;
He, the old Wrath, the Driver of Men astray,
 Pursuer of Atreus for the feast defiled;
 To assoil an ancient debt he hath paid this
  life;
A warrior and a crownèd King this day
 Atones for a slain child.

CHORUS.

—That thou art innocent herein,
 What tongue dare boast? It cannot be,
Yet from the deeps of ancient sin
 The Avenger may have wrought with thee.

—On the red Slayer crasheth, groping wild
 For blood, more blood, to build his peace again,
 And wash like water the old frozen stain
  Of the torn child.

MOURNERS.

Ah, sorrow, sorrow! My King, my King!
 How shall I weep, what word shall I say?
Caught in the web of this spider thing,
 In foul death gasping thy life away.
Woe's me, woe's me, for this slavish lying,
The doom of craft and the lonely dying,
 The iron two-edged and the hands that slay!

CLYTEMNESTRA.

And what of the doom of craft that first
He planted, making the House accurst?
What of the blossom from this root riven,
Iphigenîa, the unforgiven?
Even as the wrong was, so is the pain:
He shall not laugh in the House of the slain,
     When the count is scored;
He hath but spoilèd and paid again
     The due of the sword.

CHORUS.

I am lost; my mind dull-eyed
     Knows not nor feels
Whither to fly nor hide
     While the House reels.
The noise of rain that falls
     On the roof affrighteth me,
Washing away the walls;
     Rain that falls bloodily.

Doth ever the sound abate?
Lo, the next Hour of Fate
Whetting her vengeance due
On new whet-stones, for new
     Workings of hate.

MOURNERS.

Would thou hadst covered me, Earth, O Earth,
     Or e'er I had looked on my lord thus low,
In the pallèd marble of silvern girth!
     What hands may shroud him, what tears may
         flow?

Not thine, O Woman who dared to slay him,
Thou durst not weep to him now, nor pray
   him,
Nor pay to his soul the deep unworth
  Of gift or prayer to forget thy blow.

—Oh, who with heart sincere
  Shall bring praise or grief
To lay on the sepulchre
  Of the great chief?

CLYTEMNESTRA.

His burial is not thine to array.
  By me he fell, by me he died,
  I watch him to the grave, not cried
By mourners of his housefolk; nay,

His own child for a day like this
  Waits, as is seemly, and shall run
  By the white waves of Acheron
To fold him in her arms and kiss!

CHORUS.

Lo, she who was erst reviled
  Revileth: and what is true?
Spoil taken from them that spoiled,
  Life-blood from them that slew!
Surely while God ensueth
  His laws, while Time doth run
'Tis written: On him that doeth
  It shall be done.

This is God's law and grace,
Who then shall hunt the race
Of curses from out this hall?
The House is sealed withal
To dreadfulness.

CLYTEMNESTRA.

Aye, thou hast found the Law, and stept
In Truth's way.—Yet even now I call
The Living Wrath which haunts this hall
To truce and compact. I accept

All the affliction he doth heap
Upon me, and I charge him go
Far off with his self-murdering woe
To strange men's houses. I will keep

Some little dower, and leave behind
All else, contented utterly.
I have swept the madness from the sky
Wherein these brethren slew their kind.

[*As she ceases, exhausted and with the fire gone out
of her,* AIGISTHOS, *with Attendants, bursts
triumphantly in.*

AIGISTHOS.

O shining day, O dawn of righteousness
Fulfilled! Now, now indeed will I confess
That divine watchers o'er man's death and birth
Look down on all the anguish of the earth,
Now that I see him lying, as I love
To see him, in this net the Furies wove,
To atone the old craft of his father's hand.
  For Atreus, this man's father, in this land

Reigning, and by Thyestes in his throne
Challenged—he was his brother and mine own
Father—from home and city cast him out;
And he, after long exile, turned about
And threw him suppliant on the hearth, and won
Promise of so much mercy, that his own
Life-blood should reek not in his father's hall.
Then did that godless brother, Atreus, call,
To greet my sire—More eagerness, O God,
Was there than love!—a feast of brotherhood.
And, feigning joyous banquet, laid as meat
Before him his dead children. The white feet
And finger-fringèd hands apart he set,
Veiled from all seeing, and made separate
The tables. And he straightway, knowing naught,
Took of those bodies, eating that which wrought
No health for all his race. And when he knew
The unnatural deed, back from the board he
     threw,
Spewing that murderous gorge, and spurning brake
The table, to make strong the curse he spake:
" Thus perish all of Pleisthenês begot! "
   For that lies this man here; and all the plot
Is mine, most righteously. For me, the third,
When butchering my two brethren, Atreus spared
And cast me with my broken sire that day,
A little thing in swaddling clothes, away
To exile; where I grew, and at the last
Justice hath brought me home! Yea, though outcast
In a far land, mine arm hath reached this king;
My brain, my hate, wrought all the counselling;
And all is well. I have seen mine enemy
Dead in the snare, and care not if I die!

LEADER.

Aigisthos, to insult over the dead
I like not. All the counsel, thou hast said,
Was thine alone; and thine the will that spilled
This piteous blood. As justice is fulfilled,
Thou shalt not 'scape—so my heart presageth—
The day of cursing and the hurlèd death.

AIGISTHOS.

How, thou poor oarsman of the nether row,
When the main deck is master? Sayst thou so? . . .
To such old heads the lesson may prove hard,
I fear me, when Obedience is the word.
But hunger, and bonds, and cold, help men to find
Their wits.—They are wondrous healers of the mind!
Hast eyes and seest not this?—Against a spike
Kick not, for fear it pain thee if thou strike.

LEADER.
(turning from him to CLYTEMNESTRA).

Woman! A soldier fresh from war! To keep
Watch o'er his house and shame him in his sleep . . .
To plot this craft against a lord of spears . . .

[CLYTEMNESTRA, as though in a dream, pays no
heed. AIGISTHOS interrupts.

AIGISTHOS.

These be the words, old man, that lead to tears!
Thou hast an opposite to Orpheus' tongue,
Who chained all things with his enchanting song,
For thy mad noise will put the chains on thee.
Enough! Once mastered thou shalt tamer be.

LEADER.

Thou master? Is old Argos so accurst?
Thou plotter afar off, who never durst
Raise thine own hand to affront and strike him
    down . . .

AIGISTHOS.

To entice him was the wife's work. I was known
By all men here, his old confessed blood-foe.
Howbeit, with his possessions I will know
How to be King. And who obeys not me
Shall be yoked hard, no easy trace-horse he,
Corn-flushed. Hunger, and hunger's prison mate,
The clammy murk, shall see his rage abate.

LEADER.

Thou craven soul! Why not in open strife
Slay him? Why lay the blood-sin on his wife,
Staining the Gods of Argos, making ill
The soil thereof? . . . But young Orestes still
Liveth. Oh, Fate will guide him home again,
Avenging, conquering, home to kill these twain!

AIGISTHOS.

'Fore God, if 'tis your pleasure thus to speak and do,
    ye soon shall hear!
Ho there, my trusty pikes, advance! There cometh
    business for the spear.

    [*A body of Spearmen, from concealment outside,
    rush in and dominate the stage.*

LEADER.

Ho there, ye Men of Argos! Up! Stand and be
    ready, sword from sheath!

AIGISTHOS.

By Heaven, I also, sword in hand, am ready, and
    refuse not death!

LEADER.

Come, find it! We accept thy word. Thou offerest
    what we hunger for.

[*Some of the Elders draw swords with the Leader;
    others have collapsed with weakness. Men
    from* AGAMEMNON'S *retinue have gathered
    and prepare for battle, when, before they can
    come to blows,* CLYTEMNESTRA *breaks from
    her exhausted silence.*

CLYTEMNESTRA.

Nay, peace, O best-belovèd! Peace! And let us
    work no evil more.
Surely the reaping of the past is a full harvest, and not
    good,
And wounds enough are everywhere.—Let us not
    stain ourselves with blood.
Ye reverend Elders, go your ways, to his own
    dwelling every one,
Ere things be wrought for which men suffer.—What
    we did must needs be done.
And if of all these strifes we now may have no more,
    oh, I will kneel

And praise God, bruisèd though we be beneath the
    Daemon's heavy heel.
This is the word a woman speaks, to hear if any man
    will deign.

AIGISTHOS.

And who are these to burst in flower of folly thus of
    tongue and brain,
And utter words of empty sound and perilous,
    tempting Fortune's frown,
And leave wise counsel all forgot, and gird at him
    who wears the crown?

LEADER.

To cringe before a caitiff's crown, it squareth not
    with Argive ways.

AIGISTHOS.

(*sheathing his sword and turning from them*).

Bah, I will be a hand of wrath to fall on thee in
    after days.

LEADER.

Not so, if God in after days shall guide Orestes home
    again!

AIGISTHOS.

I know how men in exile feed on dreams . . . and
    know such food is vain.

LEADER.

Go forward and wax fat! Defile the right for this
    thy little hour!

AIGISTHOS.

I spare thee now. Know well for all this folly thou
    shalt feel my power.

LEADER.

Aye. vaunt thy greatness, as a bird beside his mate
    doth vaunt and swell.

CLYTEMNESTRA.

Vain hounds are baying round thee; oh, forget
    them! Thou and I shall dwell
As Kings in this great House. We two at last will
    order all things well.

[*The Elders and the remains of* AGAMEMNON'S
    *retinue retire sullenly, leaving the Spearmen
    in possession.* CLYTEMNESTRA *and* AIGISTHOS
    turn and enter the Palace.

NOTES TO THE AGAMEMNON

THE chief characters in the play belong to one family, as is shown by the two genealogies:—

I.

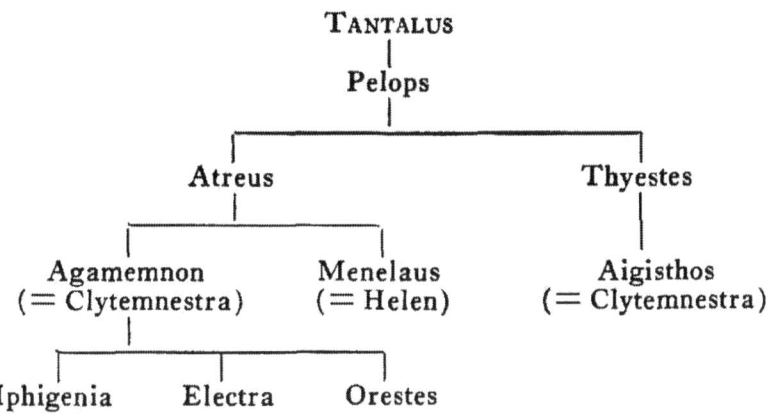

(Also, a sister of Agamemnon, name variously given, married Strophios, and was the mother of Pylades.)

II.

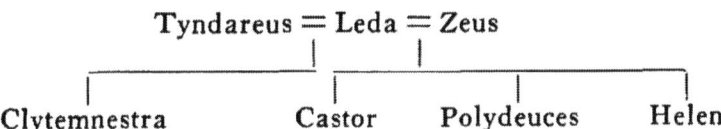

P. 1, l. 1.]—The Watchman, like most characters in Greek tragedy, comes from the Homeric tradition, though in Homer (Od. iv. 524) he is merely a servant of Aigisthos.

P. 2, l. 28, Women's triumph cry.]—This cry of the women recurs several times in the play: cf. p. 26, ll. 587 ff., p. 55, l. 1234. It is conventionally represented by "ololû"; as the cry to Apollo, Paian is "I-ê," l. 146, and Cassandra's sob is "ototoi" or "otototoi," p. 47.

Pp. 3 f., ll. 40 ff.]—With this silent scene of Clytemnestra's, compare the long silence of Cassandra below, and the silence of Prometheus in that play until his torturers have left him. See the criticism of Aeschylus in Aristophanes, *Frogs,* ll. 911–920, pp. 68, 69 in my translation.

P. 5, l. 104, Sign of the War-Way.]—i.e. an ominous sign seen by the army as it started on its journey. In Homer, Iliad, ll. 305–329, it is a snake which eats the nine young of a mother bird and then the mother, and is turned into stone afterwards.—All through this chorus the language of the prophet Calchas is intentionally obscure and riddling—the style of prophesy.

P. 7, l. 146, But I-ê, i-ê.]—(Pronounce *Ee-ay.*) Calchas, catching sight in his vision of the further consequences which Artemis will exact if she fulfils the sign, calls on Apollo Paian, the Healer, to check her.

P. 7, l. 160, Zeus, whate'er He be.]—This conception of Zeus is expressed also in Aeschylus' *Suppliant Women,* and was probably developed in the Prometheus Trilogy. See my *Rise of the Greek Epic,* p. 291 (Ed. 2).

It is connected with the common Greek conception of the *Tritos Sôtêr*—the Saviour Third. First, He who sins; next, He who avenges; third, He who saves. In vegetation worship it is the Old Year who has committed Hubris, the sin of pride, in summer; the Winter who slays him; the New Year which shall save. In mythology the three successive Rulers of Heaven are given by Hesiod as Ouranos, Kronos, Zeus (cf. *Prometheus,* 965 ff.), but we cannot tell if Aeschylus accepted the Hesiodic story. Cf. note on

l. 246, and Clytemnestra's blasphemy at l. 1387, p. 63.

P. 9, l. 192, Winds from Strymon.]—From the great river gorge of Thrace, NNE; cf. below, l. 1418.

P. 9, l. 201, Artemis.]—Her name was terrible, because of its suggestion. She demanded the sacrifice of Agamemnon's daughter, Iphigenîa. (See Euripides' two plays, *Iphigenia in Tauris* and *Iphigenia in Aulis.*) In other poets Agamemnon has generally committed some definite sin against Artemis, but in Aeschylus the death of Iphigenîa seems to be merely one of the results of his acceptance of the Sign.

P. 10, l. 215, 'Tis a Rite of old.]—Literally " it is Themis." Human sacrifice had had a place in the primitive religion of Greece; hence Agamemnon could not reject the demand of the soldiers as an obvious crime. See *Rise of Greek Epic,* pp. 150–157.

P. 11, l. 246, The Third Cup.]—Regularly poured to Zeus Sôtêr, the Saviour, and accompanied by a paean or cry of joy.

P. 11, l. 256, This Heart of Argos, this frail Tower:]—i.e. themselves.

P. 11, l. 264, Glad-voiced.]—Clytemnestra is in extreme suspense, as the return of Agamemnon will mean either her destruction or her deliverance. At such a moment there must be no ill-omened word, so she challenges fate.

P. 12, l, 276, A word within that hovereth without wings.]—i.e. a presentiment. " Winged words " are words spoken, which fly from speaker to hearer. A 'wingless' word is unspoken. The phrase occurs in Homer.

Pp. 13 ff., ll. 281 ff.]—Beacon Speech. There is no need to inquire curiously into the practical possibility of this chain of beacons. Greek tragedies do not care to be exact about this kind of detail. There may well have been a tradition that Agamemnon, like the Great King of Persia, used a chain of beacons across the Aegean.—Note how vividly Clytemnestra's imagination is working in her excitement. She seems to see before her every leaping light in the chain, just as in the next speech she imagines the scene in Troy almost with the intensity of a vision.

P. 14, l. 314, Victory in the first as in the last.]— All are Victory beacons; the spirit of Victory infects them all equally. Cf. l. 854 below, where Agamemnon prays that the Victory which is now with him, or in him, may abide.

P. 15, l. 348, A woman's word.]—Her hatred and fear of Agamemnon, making her feel vividly the horrors of the sack and the peril overhanging the conquerors, have carried her dangerously far. She checks herself and apologizes for her womanlike anxiety. Cf. l. 1661, p. 77.

P. 18, ll. 409 ff., Seers they saw visions.]—A difficult and uncertain passage. I think the seers attached to the royal household (cf. *Choëphoroe*, l. 37, where they are summoned to read a dream) were rather like what we call clairvoyants. Being consulted, they look into some pool of liquid or the like; there they see gradually emerging the palace, the injured King, the deserted room, and at last a wraith of Helen herself, haunting the place.

P. 21, l. 487.]—This break in the action, covering a space of several days, was first pointed out by Dr. Walter Headlam. Incidentally it removes the gravest of the difficulties raised by Dr. Verrall in his famous essay upon the plot of the *Agamemnon*.

P. 21, l, 495, Dry dust, own brother to the mire of war.]—i.e. " I can see by the state of his clothes, caked with dry dust which was once the mire of battle, that he comes straight from the war and can speak with knowledge." The Herald is probably (though perhaps not quite consistently) conceived as having rushed post-haste with his news.

Pp. 22 ff., HERALD.]—The Herald bursts in overcome with excitement and delight, full of love for his home and everything he sees. A marked contrast to

Agamemnon, ll. 810 ff. Note that his first speech confirms all the worst fears suggested by Clytemnestra. Agamemnon has committed all the sins she prayed against, and more. The terrible lines 527 ff., " Till her Gods' Houses, etc.," are very like a passage in *the *Persae,* 811 ff., where exactly the same acts by the Persian invaders of Greece make their future punishment inevitable.

P. 22, l. 509, Pythian Lord.]—Apollo is often a sinister figure in tragedy. Cf. Sophocles *Oedipus,* ll. 915 ff., pp. 52 f., and the similar scene, *Electra,* 655 ff. Here it is a shock to the Herald to come suddenly on the god who was the chief enemy of the Greeks at Troy. One feels Apollo an evil presence also in the Cassandra scene, ll. 1071 ff., pp. 47 ff.

P. 23, l. 530, Happy among men.]—The crown of his triumph! Early Greek thought was always asking the question, What is human happiness? To the Herald Agamemnon has achieved happiness if any one ever did. Cf. the well-known story of Croesus asking Solon who was the happiest man in the world (Herodotus, I. 30–33).

P. 24, ll. 551 ff., Herald's second speech.]—The connexion of thought is: " After all, why should either of us wish to die? All has ended well." This vivid description of the actualities of war can be better appreciated now than it could in 1913.

P. 25, l. 577, These spoils.]—Spoils purporting to come from the Trojan War were extant in Greek temples in Aeschylus' day and later.

P. 26, l. 595, Our women's joy-cry.]—There seems to have been in Argos an old popular festival, celebrating with joy or mockery the supposed death of a man and a woman. Homer (Od. iii. 309 f.) derives it from a rejoicing by Orestes over Aigisthos and Clytemnestra; cf. below, ll. 1316 ff., p. 59; Aeschylus here and Sophocles in the *Electra,* from a celebration by Clytemnestra of the deaths of Agamemnon and Cassandra. Probably it was really some ordinary New

Year and Old Year celebration to which the poets give a tragic touch. It seems to have had a woman's "Ololugmos" in it, perhaps uttered by men. See Kaibel's note, Soph. *Electra* 277–281.

P. 26, l. 612, Bronze be dyed like wool.]—Impossible in the literal sense, but there is after all a way of dying a sword red!

P. 27, l. 617, Menelaüs.]—This digression about Menelaüs is due, as similar digressions generally are when they occur in Greek plays, to the poet feeling bound to follow the tradition. Homer begins his longest account of the slaying of Agamemnon by asking "Where was Menelaüs?" (Od. iii. 249). Agamemnon could be safely attacked because he was alone. Menelaüs was away, wrecked or wind-bound.

P. 28, l. 642, Two-fold scourge.]—Ares works his will when spear crosses spear, when man meets man. Hence "two-fold."

P. 29, CHORUS. The name HELENA.]—There was a controversy in Aeschylus' day whether language, including names, was a matter of Convention or of Nature. Was it mere accident, and could you change the name of anything at will? Or was language a thing rooted in nature and fixed by God from of old? Aeschylus adopts the latter view: Why was this being called Helena? If one had understood God's purpose one would have seen it was because she really *was* "Helenâs"—*Ship-destroyer*. (The Herald's story of the shipwreck has suggested this particular idea.) Similarly, if a hero was called Aias, and came to great sorrow, one could see that he was so called from 'Aiai,' "Alas!"—The antistrophe seems to find a meaning in the name Paris or Alexandros, where the etymology is not so clear.

Pp. 33 f.]—Entrance of Agamemnon. The metre of the Chorus indicates marching; so that apparently the procession takes some time to move across the orchestra and get into position. Cassandra would be dressed, as a prophetess, in a robe of white reaching to the feet, covered by an *agrênon,* or net of wool with large meshes; she would have a staff and certain fillets or crowns. The Leader welcomes the King: he explains that, though he was against the war ten years ago, and has not changed his opinion, he is a faithful servant of the King . . . and that not all are equally so. He gave a similar hint to the Herald above, ll. 546–550, p. 24.

P. 35, Agamemnon.]—A hard, cold speech, full of pride in the earlier part, and turning to ominous threats at the end. Those who have dared to be false shall be broken.—At the end comes a note of fear, like the fear in Shakespeare's Julius Caesar. He is so full of triumph and success; he must be very careful not to provoke a fall.—Victory, Nîkê, was to the Greeks a very vivid and infectious thing. It clung to you or it deserted you. And one who was really charged with Victory, like Agamemnon, was very valuable to his friends and people. Hence they made statues of Victory wingless—so that she should not fly away. See *Four Stages of Greek Religion,* p. 138 note.

P. 36, Clytemnestra.]—A wonderful speech. It seems to me that Aeschylus' imagination realized all the confused passions in Clytemnestra's mind, but that his art was not yet sufficiently developed to make them all clear and explicit. She is in suspense; does Agamemnon know her guilt or not? At least, if she is to die, she wants to say something to justify or excuse herself in the eyes of the world. A touch of hysteria creeps in; why could he not have been killed in all these years? Why must he rise, like some monster from the grave, unkillable? Gradually she recovers her calm, explains clearly the suspicious point of Orestes' absence, and heaps up her words and gestures of welcome to an almost oriental fullness (which Agamemnon rebukes, ll. 918 ff., p. 39). Again, at the end, when she finds that for the time she is safe, her real feelings almost break out.

P. 38].—What is the motive of the Crimson

Tapestries? I think the tangling robe must have been in the tradition, as the murder in the bath certainly was. One motive, of course, is obvious: Clytemnestra is tempting Agamemnon to sin or " go too far." He tries to resist, but the splendour of an oriental homecoming seduces him and he yields. But is that enough to account for such a curious trait in the story, and one so strongly emphasized? We are told afterwards that Clytemnestra threw over her victim an " endless web," long and rich (p. 63), to prevent his seeing or using his arms. And I cannot help suspecting that this endless web was the same as the crimson pall.

If one tries to conjecture the origin of this curious story, it is perhaps a clue to realize that the word *droitê* means both a bath and a sarcophagus, or rather that the thing called droitê, a narrow stone or marble vessel about seven feet long, was in pre-classical and post-classical times used as a sarcophagus, but in classical times chiefly or solely as a bath. If among the prehistoric graves at Mycenae some later peasants discovered a royal mummy or skeleton in a sarcophagus, wrapped in a robe of royal crimson, and showing signs of violent death—such as Schliemann believed that he discovered—would they not say: " We found the body of a King murdered in a bath, and wrapped round and round in a great robe? "

P. 39 f.]—Agamemnon is going through the process of temptation. He protests rather too often and yields.

P. 39, l. 931, Tell me but this.]—This little dialogue is very characteristic of Aeschylus. Euripides would have done it at three times the length and made all the points clear. In Aeschylus the subtlety is there, but it is not easy to follow.

P. 40, l. 945, These bound slaves.]—i.e. his shoes. The metaphor shows the trend of his unconscious mind.

P. 41, l. 950, This princess.]—This is the first time

that the attention of the audience is drawn to Cassandra. She too is one of Aeschylus' silent figures. I imagine her pale, staring in front of her, almost as if in a trance, until terror seizes her at Clytemnestra's greeting in l. 1035, p. 45.

P. 41, l. 964, The cry.]—i.e. the cry of the possessed prophetess which rang from the inner sanctuary at Delphi and was intrepreted by the priests.—The last two lines of the speech are plain in their meaning but hard to translate. Literally: "when the full, or fulfilled, man walketh his home.—O Zeus the Fulfiller, fulfil my prayers."

P. 42, l. 976.]—The victim has been drawn into the house; the Chorus sing a low boding song: every audience at a Greek tragedy would expect next to hear a death cry from within, or to see a horrified messenger rush out. Instead of which the door opens and there is Clytemnestra: what does she want? "Come thou also!" One victim is not enough.—In the next scene we must understand the cause of Clytemnestra's impatience. If she stays too long outside, some one will warn Agamemnon; if she leaves Cassandra, she with her second sight will warn the Chorus. If Cassandra could only be got inside all would be safe!

P. 44, l. 1022, "One there was of old."]—Asklêpios, the physician, restored Hippolytus to life, and Zeus blasted him for so oversetting the laws of nature.

P. 45, l. 1040, Alcmêna's son.]—Heracles was made a slave to Omphalê, Queen of Lydia. His grumbles at his insufficient food were a theme of comedy.

P. 45, l. 1049, Belike thou canst not yet.]— Cf. below, ll. 1066 ff. The Elder speaks in sympathy. "Very likely you cannot yet bring yourself to submit."

P. 46, l. 1061, Thou show her.]—It seems odd to think that this passage has for centuries been translated as if it was all addressed to Cassandra:

" But if you do not understand what I say, please indicate the same with your barbarous hand!"— What makes Cassandra at last speak? I think that the Elder probably touches her, and the touch as it were breaks the spell.

P. 47, l. 1072, Cassandra.]—" Otototoi " really takes the place of a stage direction: she utters a long low sob.—The exclamation which I have trans- lated " Dreams!" seems to occur when people see ghosts or visions. *Alcestis,* 261; *Prometheus,* 567. Cf. *Phoenissae* 1296.—" Mine enemy!" The name " Apollon " suggested *" apollyon,"* Destroying . . . the form which is actually used in the Book of Revela- tion (Rev. ix. 11).

Observe how, during the lyric scene, Cassandra's vision grows steadily more definite. First vague horror of the House: then the sobbing of children, slain long ago: then, a new deed of blood coming; a woman in it: a wife: then, with a great effort, an attempt to describe the actual slaying in the bath. Lastly, the sight of herself among the slain. (This last point is greatly developed by Euripides, *Trojan Women,* ll. 445 ff., pp. 33 f.)

The story of the Children of Thyestes is given below, ll. 1590 ff., p. 73. Procnê (or Philomêla) was an Attic princess who, in fury against her Thracian husband, Têreus, killed their child Itys, or Itylus, and was changed into a nightingale, to weep for him for ever.

P. 52, ll. 1178 ff.]—Dialogue. During the lyrics Cassandra has been " possessed " or " entranced ": the turn to dialogue marks a conscious attempt to control herself and state plainly her message of warning. In order to prove her power, she first tells the Elders of deeds done in the past which are known to them but cannot have been known to her. When once they are convinced of her true seercraft, she will be able to warn them of what is coming!— The short ' stichomythia ' (line for line dialogue), dealing in awed whispers with things which can hardly be spoken, leaves the story of Cassandra still a mystery. Then her self-control breaks and the power of the God sweeps irresistibly upon her; cf. below, ll. 1256 ff., where it comes at her like a visible shape of fire, a thing not uncommon with modern clairvoyants.

P. 56, l. 1252, Thou art indeed fallen far astray.]— Because they had said " what *man*."

P. 56, l. 1265, These wreathed bands, this staff of prophesy.]—Cf. *Trojan Women,* ll. 451 ff., p. 34.

P. 60, ll. 1343 ff., The death cry; the hesitation of the Elders.]—This scene is often condemned or even ridiculed; I think, through misunderstanding. We knew the Old Men were helpless, like " dreams wandering in the day." It is essential to the story that when the crisis comes they shall be found wanting. But they are neither foolish nor cowardly; each utterance in itself is natural and characteristic, but counsels are divided. One would like to know whether Aeschylus made them speak together confusedly, as would certainly be done on the modern stage, or whether the stately conventions of Greek tragedy preferred that each speaker should finish his say. In any case, what happens is that after a moment or two of confused counsel the Elders determine to break into the Palace, but as they are mounting the steps the great doors are flung open and Clytemnestra confronts them, standing over the dead bodies of Agamemnon and Cassandra.

The illusion intended is that the Elders have entered the Palace and discovered Clytemnestra. But, as the mechanical arrangements of the Greek stage were not equal to this sudden change of scene, and since also it would, even with perfect machinery, have a tiresome interrupting effect, a slight confusion or inconsistency is allowed. We are supposed to be inside the house; but as a matter of fact the supposition is soon forgotten, and the play goes on without any attention to the particular place of the action. On Clytemnestra's speech see Introduction, p. xiii.

P. 63, l. 1387, A prayer well sped to Zeus of Hell.]—As the third gift or libation was ritually given to Zeus the Saviour, Clytemnestra blasphemously suggests that her third and unnecessary blow was an acceptable gift to a sort of anti-Zeus, a Saviour of Death.

P. 65, l. 1436, Aigisthos.]—At last the name is mentioned which has been in the mind of every one!—Chrysêïs was a prisoner of war, daughter of Chrysês, priest of Apollo. Agamemnon was made to surrender her to her father, and from this arose his quarrel with Achilles, which is the subject of the Iliad.

Pp. 67–72, ll. 1468–1573, Daemon.]—The Genius or guardian spirit of the house has in this House become a Wrath, an 'Alastor' or 'Driver Astray.' See Introduction, pp. x ff.

P. 68, l. 1513, MOURNERS.]—This attribution of the different speeches or songs to different speakers is, of course, conjectural. Ancient dramas come down to us with no stage directions and very imperfect indications of the speakers.

P. 72, l. 1579, AIGISTHOS.]—The entry of Aigisthos enlivens the scene again after the brooding and bewildered end of the dialogue between Clytemnestra and the Elders. At the same time, it seems, no doubt by deliberate intention, to reduce it to commonplace. Aigisthos' self-defence is largely justified, but he is no hero.

P. 73, l. 1602, Pleisthenês.]—Apparently one of the ancestors of Atreus, but it is not clear where he comes in the genealogy. He may be identical with Pelops.

P. 74, l. 1617. Oarsman of the nether row.]—On an ancient galley, bireme or trireme, the rowers of the lower bank of oars ranked as inferior to those who used the long oars from the deck.

P. 76, l. 1654.]—Clytemnestra, see Introduction,

p. xiii. She longs for peace, yet after all " Had Zimri peace who slew his master? " The end of the play leaves us waiting for the return of Orestes. In the first scene of the *Choëphoroe,* he is discovered standing by night at his father's grave.

Lightning Source UK Ltd.
Milton Keynes UK
UKHW021957290722
406580UK00008B/858